*Gut Yuntif, Gut Yohr*

# Gut Yuntif, Gut Yohr

by MARIE B. JAFFE

A Citadel Press Book
Published by Carol Publishing Group

First Carol Publishing Group Edition 1991

A Citadel Press Book
Published by Carol Publishing Group

Editorial Offices                     Sales & Distribution Offices
600 Madison Avenue                    120 Enterprise Avenue
New York, NY 10022                    Secaucus, NJ 07094

In Canada: Musson Book Company
A division of General Publishing Co. Limited
Don Mills, Ontario

Citadel Press is a registered trademark of
Carol Communications, Inc.

Manufactured in the United States of America
ISBN 0-8065-0390-4

Carol Publishing Group books are available at special discounts
for bulk purchases, for sales promotions, fund raising, or
educational purposes. Special editions can also be created to
specifications. For details contact: Special Sales Department,
Carol Publishing Group, 120 Enterprise Ave., Secaucus, NJ 07094

*For*
ELIAS LIEBERMAN

# CONTENTS

Let Robert Lowell, Stanley Kunitz,
Compose in English for a queen;
But me, I'll write in *mameh-loshen,*
Where competition's not so keen.

Let others think deep thoughts, and somber,
And write them down in lofty styles;
My humble mission—to bring laughter;
*Men zol zich keiklen in die aisles.*

*Gut Yuntif, Gut Yohr*

# TRANSLATIONS

# Oh Captain! My Captain!

Oh Captain, my Captain, our fearful trip is done,
The Ship has weathered every rack, the prize we sought is won;
The port is near, the bells I hear, the people all exulting,
While follow eyes the steady keel, the vessel grim and daring.

> But oh heart, heart, heart,
> Oh the bleeding drops of red,
> Where on the deck my Captain lies,
> Fallen cold and dead.

Oh Captain, my Captain, rise up and hear the bells;
Rise up—for you the flag is flung—for you the bugle trills;
For you bouquets and ribboned wreaths—for you the shores
     a-crowding,
For you they call, the swaying mass, their eager faces turning.

> Here Captain, dear Father,
> This arm beneath your head—
> It is some dream that on the deck
> You've fallen cold and dead.

My Captain does not answer, his lips are pale and still;
My father does not feel my arm, he has no pulse nor will;
The ship is anchored safe and sound, its voyage closed and
     done,
From fearful trip the victor ship comes in with object won.

> Exult oh shores, and ring oh bells,
> But I with mournful tread,
> Walk the deck my Captain lies,
> Fallen cold and dead.

WALT WHITMAN

## Kapitan! Mein Kapitan!

Kapitan, mein Kapitan! die reizeh is ge-endikt,
Die shif hot durchgelebt dem shturm,
    der tzvek is shoin guvunen;
Ot is dos land, men klingt, men ruft, men freyt zich,
    und men tumelt;
Und fun der moirediker shif nemt keyner tzu die oigen.

        Oi hartz, mein biter hartz!
        Oi roiteh tropen blut!
        Mein Kapitan ligt affen dil,
        Er ligt dort kalt und toit.

Shteh uf, mein Kapitan, und her die gloken vie zey klingen;
Shteh uf—far dir flatert der fohn, far dir blozt men dem horn;
Die blumen krantzen nor far dir; und oich der groiser oilim;
Men shtupt zich, und men zucht dir, mit neigerikeh oigen.

        Mein Kapitan, mein Tateh!
        Ich halt dir tzu dein kop!
        'Sis nor ah beyzer cholim,
        As du ligst doh kalt und toit.

Mein Kapitan, er entfert nit; die lipen bloi und shtil;
Mein Tateh veyst nit as mein orem halt ihm tzertlich tzu;
Die shift bleibt shtehn ah ruhikeh, die reizeh obgepatert;
Fun shreklichkeit kumt zie aheym, der tachlis is gevunen.

        Freyt zich oilim, gleklach klingt,
        Ober ich, mit shvereh trit,
        Mus gehen vu mein Kapitan
        Ligt dort kalt und toit.

# A Visit from St. Nicholas

"'Twas the night before Christmas, when all through the house
Not a creature was stirring, not even a mouse;
The stockings were hung by the chimney with care,
In hopes that St. Nicholas soon would be there;
The children were nestled all snug in their beds
While visions of sugar-plums danced in their heads;
And Mamma in her 'kerchief, and I in my cap,
Had just settled our brains for a long winter's nap,
When out on the lawn there arose such a clatter,
I sprang from my bed to see what was the matter.
Away to the window I flew like a flash,
Tore open the shutters and threw up the sash.
The moon on the breast of the new-fallen snow
Gave a lustre of midday to objects below,
When, what to my wondering eyes did appear,
But a miniature sleigh and eight tiny reindeer,
With a little old driver, so lively and quick,
I knew in a moment it must be St. Nick.
More rapid than eagles his coursers they came,
And he whistled, and shouted, and called them by name:
"Now, Dasher! now, Dancer! now, Prancer and Vixen!
On, Comet! on, Cupid! on, Donder and Blitzen!
To the top of the porch! to the top of the wall!
Now dash away! dash away! dash away, all!"
As dry leaves that before the wild hurricane fly,
When they meet with an obstacle, mount to the sky,
So up to the housetop the coursers they flew,
With the sleigh full of toys, and St. Nicholas too.
And then, in a twinkling, I heard on the roof
The prancing and pawing of each little hoof.
As I drew in my head, and was turning around,
Down the chimney St. Nicholas came with a bound.
He was dressed all in fur, from his head to his foot,
And his clothes were all tarnished with ashes and soot;
A bundle of toys he had flung on his back,

# Erev Krismes

'Sis geven erev krismes, und shtil is in heizel,
Kein nefeshel rirt zich, afileh kein meizel;
Beim oiveleh zeinen die zocken gehangen,
Mit hofnung as bald vet der yuntif onfangen.
Die kinderlach liegen ferdekt in die betlach,
Und zieseh choloimes bei zey tantzen in keplach;
Die veib in fatcheleh, und ich in mein yarmel—
Keh, hoben zich tzugelegt choppen ah dremil.
Don plutzling, in droisen, ah gevalt, ah gerider—
Ich shpring fun mein bet mit tzutreyselteh glider;
Ich flieh vie ah vind, ich loif ah fersamter,
Kom kom bin ich dort, und ich effen ah fenster.
Der shney hot gefallen, ah veiser, ah neier,
Und es sheint die levoneh mit herlichen feier;
Ich kuk mit berashung, ich zeh, oi vehs mir,
Ah kleinchikeh droshkeh, mit acht kleineh "reindeer";
An altinker treiber—ober freylich, geshikt,
Ich hob bald fershtannen, er muz zein Reb Nik.
Fiel shneller vie feygel, die hirshellach kummen,
Er feift, und er shreit, und er ruft zey beim nomen:
"Kum Dasher! kum Prancer! kum Dancer und Vixen!
Kum Komet! kum Kupid! kum Donder und Blitzen!
Aruf affen porch! Yetzt kricht af die vand!
Kumt, rirt zich chaveirim, zoll zein mit fershtand!"
Azoi vie fertrikenteh bletter zich hoiben,
Ven's blozt af zey shturmigeh vinten fun oiben,
Azoi is die droshkeh gefloigen tzum dach,
Mit allerlei gutinkeh zachen gepakt.
Nor ah halbeh minutkeh, in gantzen ferchoppen,
Und men hert affen dach vie die fisselach kloppen;
Ich dreh zich arum, und kom mach ich ah shtell,
Ut shteht der Reb Nikky bei mir affen shvell.
Oisgeputzt in a futter voss passt ihm zehr voil,
Ah bisseleh shmutzig mit ash und mit koil;
Shlept ah zekel mit tzatzkelach, full kein-ein-horeh,

And he looked like a peddler just opening his pack.
His eyes—how they twinkled! his dimples, how merry!
His cheeks were like roses, his nose like a cherry!
His droll little mouth was drawn up like a bow,
And the beard on his chin was as white as the snow;
The stump of a pipe he held tight in his teeth,
And the smoke, it encircled his head like a wreath;
He had a broad face and a little round belly
That shook, when he laughed, like a bowl full of jelly.
He was chubby and plump, a right jolly old elf,
And I laughed when I saw him, in spite of myself;
A wink of his eye and a twist of his head,
Soon gave me to know I had nothing to dread;
He spoke not a word, but went straight to his work,
And filled all the stockings; then turned with a jerk,
And laying his finger aside of his nose,
And giving a nod, up the chimney he rose.
He sprang to his sleigh, to his team gave a whistle.
And away they all flew like the down of a thistle.
But I heard him exclaim, ere he drove out of sight,
"HAPPY CHRISTMAS TO ALL,
AND TO ALL A GOOD-NIGHT!"

CLEMENT C. MOORE

Er kukt ois vie ah peddler vus handelt mit vareh.
Zein oigelach blischen, zein ponimel finkelt,
Die bekelach roit, und der nezel ah pinktel;
Die moil is ah kleineh, doch zehr simpatish,
Und zein shney-veiseh bord takeh gantz balebatish.
Er reychert ah lulkeh tzuvishen die tzehn,
Und der roich fliest arum zeinen kop, gradeh shehn;
Ot git er ah lach, und zein rundinker beichel,
Tzushokelt zich punkt vie ah teller mit meichel.
Ah voilinker mensheleh—gut oisgepashet,
Ich hob zich tzulacht—er hot mir nit gestrashet;
Ah vunk mit zein oig, und zein kop git ah dreh,
Men ken zich forshtellen as er is okay.
Er redt nit ah vort—zeineh arbet, ot doss,
Hot allemens zocken geshtopt ohn ah moss.
Gepotert zein arbet, dan git er ah lach,
Und hoibt zich arois, zehr shnell, durch dem dach.
Shpringt arein in zein droshkeh, ohn shtiegen, ohn leiter,
Git ah feif tzu die hirshen—ot fohren zey veiter.
Doch her ich ah shtimmeh vos zingt affen vind,
"Gut yuntif, mishpocheh, und zeits mir gezindt!"

## Lullaby

Lullaby, and good-night,
With roses bedight,
With lillies bestead
Is my baby's sweet bed.

Lay thee down now and rest,
May thy slumber be blest;
Thou shalt wake if God will,
From thy slumber so still.

JOHANNES BRAHMS

## Auld Lang Syne

Should old acquaintance be forgot,
And never brought to mind?
Should old acquaintance be forgot,
And days of old lang syne?

For old lang syne, my dear,
For old lang syne,
We'll take a cup o' kindness yet,
For old lang syne.

And here's a hand, my trusty friend,
And give us a hand of thine;
We'll take a cup o' kindness yet,
For old lang syne.

ROBERT BURNS

## Brahms' Shloflied

Ei lu lu, guteh nacht,
Mit liebeh bevacht,
Vie ah sheyn blumeleh,
Is mein kind's viegeleh.

Leyg die kepeleh tzu,
Got zol bentshen dein ruh;
Eyb der Oibershter vil,
Shloft mein kind zies und shtil.

## Dermonungen

Ver ken fargesen alteh freint,
Zey ligen in gedank,
Lomir gedenken alteh freint,
Un simches mit gezang.

Dermon zich fun die alteh teg,
Dermon zich fun amol,
L'chaim tzu die alteh teg,
Un simches fun amol.

Ot is mein hant, mein guter freint,
Un gib mir yetzt dein hant;
Lomir machen ah shnaps, mein freint,
Mit freylachs zein bekant.

## Six Haiku

NEW YEAR'S DAY

The first day of the year:
    thoughts come—and there is loneliness;
    the autumn dusk is here.

LEAVING THE HOUSE OF A FRIEND

Out comes the bee
    from deep among peony pistils—
    oh, so reluctantly!

SONG FROM THE SKY

The whole long day
    he sang, and is unsated still—
    the skylark.

THE FAMILY

Leaning upon staves
and White-haired—a whole family
visiting the graves.

THE AUTUMN OF LIFE

Nearing autumn's close,
my neighbor, now—what is it
that he does?

BASHO'S ROAD

This road:
with no man traveling on it,
autumn darkness falls.

MATSUO BASHO

## Zeks Haiku

### DER NEIER YOHR

Der ershter tog fun neien yohr—
Men tracht—'sis umetik;
Es dunkelt zich der herbst.

### AH FREINDS HOIZ

Fun tiefeh blumeleh arois,
Langzam kricht ah bien;
Er vil dos naches nit ferlozen.

### LIED FUN HIMEL

Ah gantzen tog flieht der foigel,
Und zingt tzum himel;
Und zingt, und vil nit oifheren.

### DIE MISHPOCHEH

Die gantzeh groyeh mishpocheh—
Yeder lehnt zich af ah shteken—
Kumt bezuchen dem beys oilim.

### TZUM SOF FUN LEBEN

Mein shochen, azoi nohnt tzum herbst—
Vos tut er dorten
Mit zein leben?

### DER EINZAMER VEG

Mein veg—men zeht nit
Keyn neshomeh;
Bald vet mein tog fergehn.

## To My Brothers Everywhere

Test me not for shibboleth;
      Like a king, anointed, ermined,
I was born into a faith
      And my skin was predetermined.

Bearing burdens on my back
      You will find me everywhere;
Tropic suns have turned me black,
      Northern winds have bleached me fair.

But the heart within me beats
      Just like yours in utter blindness
To the rhythm of the streets
      To an act of hate or kindness.

Though my house be paradise,
      Every wall is made of glass;
May the question in my eyes
      Brush your spirit as I pass.

By the sacrament of pain
      Men must share with one another,
By the hopes we nursed in vain
      You will know me, O my brother.

ELIAS LIEBERMAN

## Tzu Meineh Brider Umetum

Du zolst mir nit prubiren mit shiboilehs;
Vie ah kenig yarshendik zein kroin,
Hob ich geyarshent mein amuneh,
Und mein kolir hot Got bezorgt.

Du vest mir umetum gefinen—
Der shverer last af meineh pleytzes;
In heyseh lender hot die zun fershvartzt;
Die kalteh tzofen vinten, blas gemacht.

Doch klapt mein hartz azoi vie deins,
In blindeh gramen hamert es;
Es vert fertzart mit has und shlechts;
Die liebshaft leitert es mit freyd.

Afileh is mein heym g'n eyden,
Die vent zeinen fun gloz gemacht;
Begegendik, zol dein neshomeh
Fun meinem blik veren ervacht.

Veil aleh leiden mir tzuzamen,
Und deineh tzorehs zeinen meineh;
Oich unzereh umzisteh hofnung—
Du vest mir shoin derkennen, bruder.

# The Owl and the Pussy-Cat

The Owl and the Pussy-Cat went to sea
    In a beautiful pea-green boat,
They took some honey, and plenty of money
    Wrapped up in a five-pound note.
The Owl looked up to the stars above,
    And sang to a small guitar,
"O lovely Pussy, O Pussy, my love,
    What a beautiful Pussy you are,
        You are,
        You are!
    What a beautiful Pussy you are!"

Pussy said to the Owl, "You elegant fowl,
    How charmingly sweet you sing!
Oh! let us be married, too long we have tarried:
    But what shall we do for a ring?"
They sailed away, for a year and a day,
    To the land where the Bong-tree grows;
And there in a wood a Piggy-wig stood,
    With a ring at the end of his nose,
        His nose,
        His nose,
    With a ring at the end of his nose.

"Dear Pig, are you willing to sell for one shilling
    Your ring?" Said the Piggy, "I will."
So they took it away, and were married next day
    By the Turkey who lives on the hill.

## Die Eyleh und Die Ketzeleh

Die eyleh und die ketzeleh zeinen obgeforen
In ah shifeleh sheyn und grin;
Zich bevorent mit honig, und ah zekeleh gelt,
Alts guts vos kumt affen zin.
Die eyleh kukt tzu die shtern aruf,
Und zingt fun ah fullen hartz,
"Oi ketzeleh meins, vie sheyn du bist,
Ich hob dir azoi fiel lieb,
     'Ch hob dir lieb,
Veil du bist azoi cheynevdig sheyn."


Zie git ihm an entfer, "Mein teierer freind,
Dein shtimmeh vie tzuker is zies;
Af vos darf men varten? Lommir shtellen ah chupeh—
Ober vu ken men koifen ah ring?"
Is men veiter gefohren, ah hibsh bissel tzeit,
Bis men kumt tzu ah land mit groz;
Und dorten beim breg ah chazerl shteht,
Und es hengt ihm ah ring affen noz,
     Fun zein noz,
Takeh hengt dort ah ring fun zein noz.


"Guter mentsh, tuh ah toiveh, dein ringel farkoif"—
Dem chazerl hot es geloint;
Es veist takeh ois, as die simcheh is grois;
Nu, zol zein mit mahzel und glik.

They dined on mince and slices of quince,
    Which they ate with a runcible spoon;
And hand in hand, on the edge of the sand,
    They danced by the light of the moon,
      The moon,
      The moon,
    They danced by the light of the moon.

                  EDWARD LEAR

## Serenade

Stars of the summer night!
Far in yon azure deeps,
Hide, hide your golden light!
She sleeps, my lady sleeps.

Moon of the summer night!
Far down yon western steeps,
Sink, sink in silver light!
She sleeps, my lady sleeps.

Wind of the summer night!
Where yonder woodbine creeps,
Fold, fold thy pinions light!
She sleeps, my lady sleeps.

Dreams of the summer night!
Tell her, her lover keeps
Watch, while in slumber light,
She sleeps, my lady sleeps.

    HENRY WADSWORTH LONGFELLOW

Men hot zich balekt fun die besteh maicholim,
Men hot kiddush gemacht mit vein;
Und ah lebedig tentzel gechapt affen zamd,
Die levoneh hot zey tzugesheint,
    Lichtig gesheint,
Hot lichtig gemacht zeyer tantz.


## Ovend Muzik

Shterner in zumer nacht,
Veit in dem himel bloi,
Behalt dem golden licht—
Zie shloft, mein dameh shloft.

Levoneh in zumer nacht,
Dorten in meirev-zeit,
Zink in dein zilber licht—
Zie shloft, mein dameh shloft.

Vint in der zumer nacht,
Dort vu der boimel vaxt,
Pamelach, stiler bloz—
Zie shloft, mein dameh shloft.

Troimeh in zumer nacht,
Zogt ihr, ihr liebster vacht,
Hiet ihr ah gantzeh nacht—
Zie shloft, mein dameh shloft.

# Hiawatha's Childhood

By the shores of Gitche Gumee,
By the shining Big-Sea-Water,
Stood the wigwam of Nokomis,
Daughter of the Moon, Nokomis.
Dark behind it rose the forest,
Rose the black and gloomy pine-trees,
Rose the firs with cones upon them;
Bright before it beat the water,
Beat the clear and sunny water,
Beat the shining Big-Sea-Water.

There the wrinkled, old Nokomis
Nursed the little Hiawatha.
Rocked him in his linden cradle,
Bedded soft in moss and rushes,
Safely bound with reindeer sinews;
Stilled his fretful wail by saying,
"Hush! the Naked Bear will hear thee!"
Lulled him into slumber, singing,
"Ewa-yea! my little owlet!
Who is this, that lights the wigwam?
With his great eyes lights the wigwam?
Ewa-yea! my little owlet!"

Many things Nokomis taught him
Of the stars that shine in heaven;
Showed him Ishkoodah, the comet,
Ishkoodah, with fiery tresses;
Showed the Death-Dance of the spirits,
Warriors with their plumes and war-clubs,
Flaring far away to northward
In the frosty nights of Winter;
Showed the broad, white road in heaven,
Pathway of the ghosts, the shadows,
Running straight across the heavens,
Crowded with the ghosts, the shadows.

## Die Kindheit Fun Hiawatha

Bei dem breg fun Gitche-Gumee,
Bei dem blischendiken vasser,
Shteyt die heiskeh fun Nokomis,
Tochterel fun der Levoneh.
Hinter diezen vigvam-heiskeh,
Vaxt ah vald, gedicht mit boimer,
Hoicheh, shvartzeh, shtilleh boimer;
Und in forent shlogt der vasser,
Klor und zunig is der vasser,
Blischet vie ah yam, der vasser.

Dort die altichkeh Nokomis
Hodevet dem Hiawatha,
Shokelt tzu dem kleinem nefesh,
In zein vigeleh—geflochten
Azoi veych, und shtark, und varem;
Shtilt ihm ein ven er tzuveynt zich,
"Shah, der ber zoll dir nit heren."
Zie fershloft ihm mit ah liedel,
"Ewa-yea, mein kleyner foigel,
Ver is dos, vos macht dem vigvam
Azoi lichtig mit zein oigen?
Ewa-yea, mein kleyner foigel!"

Zie hot ihm asach gelerent
Fun die helleh shtern in himmel;
Vie zey heysen, vos zey tuhen;
Ishkoodah, dos is ah komet;
Hot ihm ongetzeigt die braveh,
Die neshomehs fun die helden,
Vie dem Tantz-fun-Toit zey tantzen,
In die kalteh necht fun vinter;
Hot ihm ongetzeigt dem breiten,
Veissen veg, vos loift in himmel,
Vu die shottens und neshomehs,
Shtoissen zich tzu gehn ariber.

[27]

At the door on summer evenings
Sat the little Hiawatha;
Heard the whispering of the pine-trees,
Heard the lapping of the water,
Sounds of music, words of wonder;
"Minne-wawa!" said the pine-trees,
"Mudway-aushka!" said the water.

Saw the fire-fly, Wah-wah-taysee,
Flitting through the dusk of evening,
With the twinkle of its candle
Lighting up the brakes and bushes,
And he sang the song of children,
Sang the song Nokomis taught him:
"Wah-wah-taysee, little fire-fly,
Little, flitting, white-fire insect,
Little, dancing, white-fire creature,
Light me with your little candle,
Ere upon my bed I lay me,
Ere in sleep I close my eyelids!"

Saw the moon rise from the water,
Rippling, rounding from the water,
Saw the flecks and shadows on it,
Whispered, "What is that, Nokomis?"
And the good Nokomis answered:

"Once a warrior, very angry,
Seized his grandmother, and threw her
Up into the sky at midnight;
Right against the moon he threw her;
'Tis her body that you see there."

Saw the rainbow in the heaven,
In the eastern sky, the rainbow,
Whispered, "What is that, Nokomis?"
And the good Nokomis answered:

Affen shvell, in zummer nechten,
Zitzt der kleyner Hiawatha;
Hert die boimer, vie zey shushken,
Hert dem vasser, vie er plushket,
Zieser nigun, vunder-verter;
"Minne-wawa," fun die boimer,
"Mudway-aushka!" zogt der vasser.

Zeht dem feier-flig, Wah-wah-taysee,
Vie er flieht ferbai in ovent,
Mit zein funkeldigen lichtel,
Macht er lichtig als arumet;
Und er zingt ah kinder-liedel,
Vos Nokomis ihm gelerent:
"Wah-wah-taysee, kleineh feier-flig,
Klieneh flig mit veissen feier,
Kleineh tantzendigeh nefesh,
Mach mir lichtig mit dein lichtel,
Eyder ich leyg zich in bettel,
Eyder ich fermach die oigen!"

Zeht vie die levoneh heybt zich,
Rund es kumt arois fun vasser,
Zeht die shotens und die flecken,
Fregt er, "Vos is dos, Nokomis?"
Und die guteh alteh entfert:

" 'Sis geven amol ah yeger,
Hot tzukrigt zich mit zein bobeh,
Mit grois kas hot ihr gevorfen
Gleich aruf tzu der levoneh;
Vos du zehst dort, is ihr kerper."

Zeht dem regen-boigen oiben,
In dem himmel, in dem mizrach,
Fregt er, "Vos is dos, Nokomis?"
Und die guteh alteh entfert:

"'Tis the heaven of flowers you see there;
All the wild flowers of the forest,
All the lilies of the prairie,
When on earth they fade and perish,
Blossom in that heaven above us."

When he heard the owls at midnight,
Hooting, laughing in the forest,
"What is that?" he cried in terror;
"What is that?" he said, "Nokomis?"
And the good Nokomis answered:
"That is but the owl and owlet,
Talking in their native language,
Talking, scolding at each other."

Then the little Hiawatha
Learned of every bird its language,
Learned their names and all their secrets,
How they built their nests in Summer,
Where they hid themselves in Winter.
Talked with them whene'er he met them,
Called them "Hiawatha's Chickens."

Of all beasts he learned the language,
Learned their names and all their secrets,
How the beavers built their lodges,
Where the squirrels hid their acorns,
How the reindeer ran so swiftly,
Why the rabbit was so timid,
Talked with them whene'er he met them,
Called them "Hiawatha's Brothers."

HENRY WADSWORTH LONGFELLOW

"Du zehst dort ah blumen-himmel;
Alleh blumen fun dem vald, und
Alleh blumen fun die felder,
Ven af unzer erd zey shtarben,
Bliehen noch amol in himmel."

Ven er hert bei nacht, die aileh,
Vie zey kvitchen mit gelechter,
Vert er zehr shtark dershroken;
"Vos is dos, Nokomis?" shreit er.
Und die guteh alteh entfert:
"Dos is nur ah por nacht-foigel,
Reden zey in mameh-loshen,
Shreien, shilten, ains dem andern."

Dan der kleiner Hiawatha,
Lernt yeden foigel-loshen,
Vert bekant mit zeiereh nemen,
Und mit alleh zeiereh vegen,
Vie zey boiyen zummer nesten,
Vu zey kleiben zich in vinter;
Ruft zey "Hiawatha's Hiener."

Vert bekant mit alleh chaies,
Zeier loshen, nemen, vegen;
Vie die bibers boiyen lagers,
Veviorkehs behalten nislach,
Vu die shnelleh hirshen loifen,
Farvos kroliks hoben moireh;
Redt zich ois mit zey tzuzammen;
Ruft zey "Hiawatha's Brider."

## Believe Me if All Those Endearing Young Charms

Believe me if all those endearing young charms,
Which I gaze on so fondly today,
Were to change by tomorrow, and fleet in my arms,
Like fairy gifts fading away.
Thou wouldst still be adored, as this moment thou art,
Let thy loveliness fade as it will,
And around the dear ruin each wish of my heart
Would entwine itself verdantly still.

It is not while beauty and youth are thine own,
And thy cheeks unprofaned by a tear,
That the fervour and faith of a soul can be known,
To which time will but make thee more dear.
No, the heart that has truly loved never forgets,
But as truly loves on to the close;
As the sun-flower turns on her god, when he sets,
The same look which she turned when he rose.

THOMAS MOORE

## Gloib Mir

Gloib mir, as afileh ven dein yunger cheyn,
Velcher heint git mir naches und freyd,
Vet zein morgen fereltert, dein reitz vet fergehn,
Azoi vie alts veltlich fergeht.

Bei mir vest du immer zein teier vie gold,
Chotsh fervelkt, und die lipen nit roit;
Veil der churben, der lieber, is deins—hob ich's holt,
Und ich bleib dir getrei biz dem toit.

'Sis nit nur ven sheynheit und yugend is dein,
Und du host nit fergossen ah trer—
As men zeht dan vie gut die neshomeh ken zein;
Mit der tzeit vert es teierer, mehr.

Neyn, dos hartz vos hot emes geliebt, zie gedenkt,
Und zie liebt biz der otem geht ois;
Punkt azoi vie ah blumeleh noch die zun benkt—
Ven er hoibt zich, oich ven er geht ois.

## Clementine

In a cavern, in a canyon,
Excavating for a mine,
Dwelt a miner, Forty-niner,
And his daughter Clementine.

Light she was, and like a fairy,
And her shoes were number nine,
Herring-boxes, without topses,
Sandals were for Clementine.

Drove she ducklings, to the water,
Every morning just at nine,
Hit her foot against a splinter,
Fell into the foaming brine.

Ruby lips above the water,
Blowing bubbles soft and fine,
Alas for me, I was no swimmer,
So I lost my Clementine.

> Oh my darling, oh my darling,
> Oh my darling Clementine,
> You are lost and gone forever,
> Dreadful sorry, Clementine.

PERCY MONTROSE

## Klementein

In ah groiseh hoil dort ergetz,
Vu men grobt dort in ah mein,
Voint ah meiner mit zein tochter,
Und men ruft ihr Klementein.

Leicht is zie und vie ah feder,
Ihreh shichlach numer nine;
Ihreh tuflehs zeinen kestelach,
Oi, is dos ah Klementein.

Yeden tog um nein ahzeyger,
Treibt zie katshkelach tzum teich;
Hot getrofen dort ahn umglik,
In dem vasser falt zie gleich.

Zeht men lipelach in vasser,
Blozen in der velt arein;
Oi, ah broch, ich ken nit shvimen,
Is ferfallen Klementein.

Oi mein teiereh, mein zieseh,
Mein gelibteh Klementein,
Bist avek fun mir af eybig;
Veh is mir, mein Klementein

# My Shadow

I have a little shadow that goes in and out with me,
And what can be the use of him is more than I can see.
He is very, very like me from the heels up to the head;
And I see him jump before me, when I jump into my bed.

The funniest thing about him is the way he likes to grow—
Not at all like proper children, which is always very slow;
For he sometimes shoots up taller like an India-rubber ball,
And he sometimes gets so little that there's none of him at all.

He hasn't got a notion of how children ought to play,
And can only make a fool of me in every sort of way.
He stays so close beside me, he's a coward you can see;
I'd think shame to stick to nursie as that shadow sticks to me!

One morning, very early, before the sun was up,
I rose and found the shining dew on every buttercup;
But my lazy little shadow, like an arrant sleepy-head,
Had stayed at home behind me and was fast asleep in bed.

ROBERT LOUIS STEVENSON

## Mein Shoten

Ich hob ah kleynem shoten vos is tzugeklept tzu mir,
Af vos ich ken ihm nutzen, is ah groiser sod bei mir.
Er is zehr tzu mir enlich, fun die fis biz dem kop mein;
Und ven ich leyg zich shlofen, shpringt er gleich in bet arein.

Die zach vos macht ihm komish, is vie der shoten vaxt—
Nit vie emeseh kinder vaxen, gants pavoliyeh, und gelas;
Amol tzieht er zich fernander, is er lang vie viorsten tzehn;
Und amol vert er azoi kurtz, as men ken ihm bald nit zehn.

Vie kinder darfen shpielen, ot dos ken er nit fershtehn,
Macht er imer fun mir choizik, vie ah yederer ken zehn.
Er is azah shrekediker, er lost mir nit tzuruh;
Ich volt zich shemen azoi shtendig mameh's fartach halten tzu.

Eyn mol, in ah frimorgen, eyder die zun hot zich gerirt,
Bin ich shtil arois fun hois, tzu die blumen zich gefirt;
Mein kleyner krumer shoten, zein foilkeit azoi grois,
Is gebliben shtark farshlofen, und is nit fun bet arois.

# The Village Blacksmith

Under a spreading chestnut tree
The village smithy stands;
The smith, a mighty man is he,
With large and sinewy hands;
And the muscles of his brawny arms
Are strong as iron bands.

His hair is crisp and black and long,
His face is like the tan;
His brow is wet with honest sweat,
He earns whate'er he can,
And looks the whole world in the face,
For he owes not any man.

Week in, week out, from morn till night,
You can hear his bellows blow;
You can hear him swing his heavy sledge,
With measured beat and slow,
Like a sexton ringing the village bell,
When the evening sun is low.

And children coming home from school
Look in at the open door;
They love to see the flaming forge,
And hear the bellows roar,
And catch the burning sparks that fly
Like chaff from a threshing floor.

He goes on Sunday to the church,
And sits among his boys;
He hears the parson pray and preach,
He hears his daughter's voice,
Singing in the village choir,
And it makes his heart rejoice.

## Der Shmid Fun Dorf

Unter ahn oisgeshpreyten boim,
Die shmiderei dort shteyt;
Der shmid, ah zehr shtarker man,
Mit groiseh, grobeh hent;
Die orems zeineh, punkt azoi
Vie bender eizerneh.

Die hor fun kop is shvartz un lang,
Zein ponim is farbrent;
Der shtern farshveitst fun horeven,
Zein cheylik gut fardient;
Un kukt eich gleich in ponim ein,
Ahn orentlicher mentsh.

Voch ein, voch ois, fun frieh biz nacht,
Die bloz-zek ken men hern;
Dem shmidhamer git er ah zets,
Ahn oisgemostenem;
Azoi hert men dem glok fun dorf,
Ven die ovent zun fargeht.

Un kinder kumendik aheym,
Kuken in tier arein;
Zey zeinen shtark interisirt
In bloz-zak, un in flam;
Zey chapen funken mit die hent,
Vie s'volt zein kernlach.

Zuntig geht er in kirch arein,
Un zitst mit zeineh zien;
Er hert dem galach preydiken,
Dem zingen fun dem chor;
Darkent zein tochter's ziesen kol—
Zein hartz mit freyd is ful.

It sounds to him like her mother's voice,
Singing in Paradise!
He needs must think of her once more,
How in the grave she lies;
And with his hard, rough hand he wipes
A tear out of his eyes.

Toiling, rejoicing, sorrowing,
Onward through life he goes;
Each morning sees some task begun,
Each evening sees it close;
Something attempted, something done,
Has earned a night's repose.

Thanks, thanks to thee, my worthy friend,
For the lesson thou hast taught!
Thus at the flaming forge of life
Our fortunes must be wrought;
Thus on its sounding anvil shaped,
Each burning deed and thought!

HENRY WADSWORTH LONGFELLOW

Es dacht zich vie ihr muter's kol
Zingt in ganeydn mit;
Dermont zich fun zein lieber veib,
Vos in ihr keyver ligt;
Un mit zein harteh, grobeh hant,
Visht er ah trer fun oig.

Er horevet mit zorg, mit freyd,
Azoi geht zich dos leben;
Friemorgen shtelt zich arbeten,
Un fartig is in ovent;
Er hot zein flicht gut opgetohn,
Zein shlof hot er fardient.

Ah sheynem dank dir, lieber freint,
Du host uns gut gelernt;
As bei dem lebens heysen flam,
Muz yeder zich bemiehen;
Un yedeh mitzvoh vos men tuht,
Zol zein ahn emesdikeh.

## Old Smoky

On top of Old Smoky, all covered with snow,
I lost my true lover, a-courting too slow.
Now courting is pleasure, and parting is grief,
But a false-hearted lover, is worse than a thief.

A thief he will rob you, and take what you have,
But a false-hearted lover, will take you to your grave.
The grave will decay you, and turn you to dust—
But where is the young man, a poor girl can trust?

They'll hug you and kiss you, and tell you more lies,
Than the cross-ties on railroads, or stars in the skies.
They'll tell you they love you, to give your heart ease,
But the minute your back's turned, they'll court
          whom they please.

On top of Old Smoky, all covered with snow,
I lost my true lover, by courting too slow.
Bury me on Old Smoky, Old Smoky so high,
Where the wild birds in heaven, can hear my sad cry.

## Alter Smoky

Affen shpitz Alten Smoky, beshoten mit shney,
Dort hob ich ferloiren mein liebsten, oi veh!
Ferliebt zein is naches, tzu sheiden is shmertz—
Ah falsher geliebter hot tzubrochen mein hertz.

Ah ganif beganvet, er nemt vos is dein,
Ober ah falsher geliebter treibt in keyver arein.
Der keyver ferdarbt dir, und macht fun dir shtoiben—
Gefint zich ah yungatsch vos ah meydel ken gloiben?

Zey tzertlen und kushen, du bist bei zey gern,
Zey zogen dir ligens, fiel mehr, vie 'sis shtern.
Zey shveren dir liebeh, du fielst ah mechayeh—
Nur dreh zich arumet, ot hot er ah neieh.

Affen shpitz Alten Smoky, beshoten mit shney,
Dort hob ich ferloiren mein liebsten, oi veh!
Begrobt mir bei Smoky, er is hoich, er is vahr—
Dort velen di feygel kenen heren mein tzar.

## Fable

The mountain and the squirrel
Had a quarrel.
And the former called the latter, Little Prig.
Bun replied—"You are doubtless very big;
But all sorts of things and weather
Must be taken in together
To make up a year and a sphere;
And I think it no disgrace
To occupy my place;
If I'm not so large as you,
You are not so small as I,
And not half so spry:
I'll not deny you make
A very pretty squirrel track;
Talents differ; all is well and wisely put.
If I cannot carry forests on my back,
Neither can you crack a nut."

RALPH WALDO EMERSON

## Ah Meisseleh

Der barg und die veviorkeh
Hoben zich tzukrigt,
Und der ershter ruft die tzveyteh,
"Kleyner Gornisht."
Git zie ihm an entfer—
"Du bist takeh zehr grois;
Ober allerlei umshtenden kumen zich tzuzamen
Obtzurichten ah yohr und ah velt.
Und ich shem zich takeh nit
Tzu fernemen mein platz.
Oib ich bin nit azoi grois vie du,
Bist du nit azoi kleyn vie ich—
Und takeh nit azoi lebedig.
Ich gib dir tzu, as du machst
Ah zehr sheynem shpur far veviorkehs;
'Sfaran allerlei talanten af der velt;
Yeder eyner hot zich zein ort und zein tachlis.
Ich ken takeh nit shlepen ah vald af die pleytzes—
Und du kenst nit tzuknaken ah nissel."

# The Bells

Hear the sledges with the bells—silver bells!
What a world of merriment their melody fortells!
How they tinkle, tinkle, tinkle,
In the icy air of night,
While the stars that oversprinkle
All the heavens, seem to twinkle
With a crystalline delight;
Keeping time, time, time,
In a sort of runic rhyme,
To the tintinabulation that so musically wells
From the bells, bells, bells, bells,
      Bells, bells, bells—
From the jingling and the tinkling of the bells.

Hear the mellow wedding bells—golden bells!
What a world of happiness their harmony fortells!
Through the balmy air of night,
How they ring out their delight!
From the molten golden notes,
And all in tune,
What a liquid ditty floats,
To the turtle-dove that listens, while she gloats
On the moon!
Oh, from out the sounding cells,
What a gush of euphony voluminously wells!
How it swells, how it dwells
On the future! how it tells
Of the rapture that impells
To the swinging and the ringing
Of the bells, bells, bells—
Of the bells, bells, bells, bells,
      Bells, bells, bells—
To the rhyming and the chiming of the bells!

## Die Gloken

Her die shliten glekelach—zilberneh—
Azah freylichkeit zey shpielen;
Vie zey klingen, klingen, klingen,
In die kalteh luft fun nacht,
Un die shternlach vos finklen,
Mit ah kalten fargenigen,
In dem himel ful mit pracht.
Vie zey halten op dem takt,
Vie zey tzelen op dem gram,
Vie zey klingen, vie zey zingen,
Azah ziesen tararam.
Sheyneh glekelach vos shpielen,
Ah geshmaken tararam.

Her die chupeh glekelach—goldeneh—
Azah gliklichkeit zey shpielen,
Azah sholem, azah freyd;
In die varmeh luft fun nacht,
Vie zey klingen mit hanoieh,
Mit ah shtimeh goldeneh,
Mit ah nigun hartzlicheh;
Zey foroiszogen die tzukunft,
In ah mazeldikeh shoh.
Un die glekelach, zey klingen,
Un die glekelach, zey zingen,
Un die velt is ful mit naches,
Ot oh doh.

Her die shreiedikeh gloken—kuperneh—
Azah moireh, azah shrek, shturmen zey;
In die tziterikeh nacht,
Vie zey tumlen, vie zey reisen,
Vie zey machen ah gevalt;

Hear the loud alarum bells—brazen bells—
What a tale of terror, now their turbulency tells!
In the startled ear of night
How they scream out their affright!
Too much horrified to speak,
They can only shriek, shriek,
Out of tune,
In a clamorous appealing to the mercy of the fire,
In a mad expostulation with the deaf and frantic fire,
Leaping higher, higher, higher,
With a desperate desire,
And a resolute endeavor
Now—now to sit, or never,
By the side of the pale-faced moon.
Oh the bells, bells, bells,
What a tale their terror tells, of Despair!
How they clang, and clash, and roar!
What a horror they outpour
On the bosom of the palpitating air!
Yet the ear, it fully knows,
By the twanging, and the clanging,
How the danger ebbs and flows;
Yet the ear distinctly tells,
In the jangling, and the wrangling,
How the danger sinks and swells,
By the sinking or the swelling in the anger of the bells—
Of the bells, bells, bells, bells, bells—
In the clamor and the clangor of the bells!

Hear the tolling of the bells—iron bells!
What a world of solemn thought their monody compells!
In the silence of the night,
How we shiver with affright
At the melancholy menace of their tone!
For every sound that floats
From the rust within their throats,
Is a groan.

[48]

Nor zey shreien, shreien, shreien—
Vie zey liarmen, un zey beten—
Hob rachmonehs—fun dem feier—
Beten baremhartzikeit, fun feier.
Un der feier shpringt als hecher,
Hecher, hecher shpringt der feier—
Veil er vil, nit andersh, zitsen
Bei der zeit fun der levoneh.
Oi die gloken, gloken, gloken,
Vie fun toitshrek kvitshen zey,
Af die klogedikeh luft.
Un der oier ken farshtehn,
Ken oistzeichnen, ken darkenen
Vie geferlich is der feier—
Vie es brent—
Fun die shreiedikeh gloken,
Fun die liarmen,
Fun die shturmen,
Fun die gloken vos gevaldeven azoi.

Her die klungen fun die gloken—eizerneh—
Azah troirigkeit der kloglied brengt tzu uns—
In der shtilkeit fun der nacht,
Vie mir tziteren fun shrek—
Un die moiredikeh tener strashen uns.
Yeder klang vos shvebt aher,
Fun dem zhaver in die heldzer,
Is ah krechts.
Un die mentshelach vos voinen
In dem kloister-turem oiben, gants aleyn—
Ven zey klingen, klingen, klingen
In azah fardushten tohn,
Ongetzunden mit entzikung,
Keiklen zey in hartz ah shteyn—
Oif die hertzer fun die mentshen ligt ah shteyn.
Ot die mentshelach dort oiben—

And the people—ah, the people—
They that dwell up in the steeple, all alone,
And who tolling, tolling, tolling,
In that muffled monotone,
Feel a glory in so rolling
On the human heart a stone—
They are neither man nor woman—
They are neither brute nor human—
They are ghouls:
And their king it is who tolls—
As he rolls, rolls, rolls, rolls
A paen from the bells!
And his merry bosom swells
With the paean of the bells!
And he dances, and he yells;
Keeping time, time, time,
In a sort of runic rhyme,
To the paean of the bells—
Keeping time, time, time,
In a sort of runic rhyme,
To the throbbing of the bells—
Of the bells, bells, bells,
To the sobbing of the bells;
Keeping time, time, time,
As he knells, knells, knells,
In a happy runic rhyme,
To the rolling of the bells—
Of the bells, bells, bells—
To the tolling of the bells—
Of the bells, bells, bells, bells—
To the moaning and the groaning of the bells.

EDGAR ALLAN POE

'Sis nit mener, un nit froien,
Un afileh nit keyn chaies—
Sheydim zeinen zey.
Un der meylach fun die briehs,
Er is dos vos halt in klingen—
Ven er keikelt, keikelt, keikelt—
Ven er vikelt ois die tener
Fun die gloken.
Er hot groisen fargenigen
Fun die troierikeh tener
Fun die gloken.
Un er hotzket un er tantzt,
Un er kvitshet, un er shreit,
Er geht gradeh mit dem takt
Fun die gloken—
Die pulsirendikeh gloken,
Fun die hershendikeh gloken,
Fun die gloken velcheh klingen
Noch ah toidt.

# Mandalay

By the old Mulmein Pagoda,
Looking eastward to the sea,
There's a Burma girl a-setting,
And I know she thinks of me;
For the wind is in the palm-trees,
And the temple-bells they say:
"Come you back, you British soldier;
Come you back to Mandalay!"

> Come you back to Mandalay,
> Where the old flotilla lay:
> Can't you hear their paddles chunking,
> From Rangoon to Mandalay?
> On the road to Mandalay,
> Where the flying fishes play,
> And the dawn comes up like thunder
> Outer China 'crost the Bay!

Ship me somewhere east of Suez,
Where the best is like the worst,
Where there ain't no Ten Commandments,
And a man can raise a thirst;
For the temple-bells are calling,
And it's there that I would be—
By the old Mulmein Pagoda,
Looking lazy at the sea.

> On the road to Mandalay,
> Where the old flotilla lay,
> With our sick beneath the awnings,
> When we went to Mandalay;

# FUN
## *Mandalay*

Bei der alt' Mulmein Pagoda,
Bei der alter mizrach tir,
Zitst ah meydeleh fun Burma,
Un ich veys zie tracht fun mir;
Veil ah vintel blozt die beymer,
Zingen glekelach, "Oi vey,
Kum tzurik, soldat-fun-England,
Kum tzurik tzu Mandalay!"

    Kum tzurik tzu Mandalay,
    Vu die alteh shifen shtehn;
    Du kenst hern ruders drehen,
    Fun Rangoon biz Mandalay;
    Af dem veg tzu Mandalay,
    Fliehen fishlach azoi sheyn;
    Der frimorgen kumt vie duner
    Fun dem vaser bei Chineh.

Ich vil gehn tzurik tzu Suez,
Dorten zeinen aleh fein;
Dort' nitoh keyn tzehn geboten,
Un ver's vil, ken shiker zein;
Temple-glekelach, zey rufen,
Dorten hot dos leben tam,
Bei der alt' Mulmein Pagoda,
Vil ich kuken afen yam.

    Af dem veg tzu Mandalay,
    Vu die alteh shifen shteyn;
    Men fardekt die krankeh chevreh,
    Forendik tzu Mandalay;

On the road to Mandalay,
Where the flying fishes play,
And the dawn comes up like thunder,
Outer China 'crost the Bay!

RUDYARD KIPLING

## *Who Is Sylvia?*

Who is Silvia? what is she,
That all our swains commend her?
Holy, fair and wise is she;
The heavens such grace did lend her,
That she might admired be,
That she might admired be.

Is she kind as she is fair?
For beauty lives with kindness.
Love doth to her eyes repair,
To help him of his blindness,
And being helped, inhabits there,
And being helped, inhabits there.

Then to Silvia let us sing,
That Silvia is excelling;
She excells each mortal thing,
Upon the dull earth dwelling;
To her let us garlands bring,
To her let us garlands bring.

WILLIAM SHAKESPEARE

Af dem veg tzu Mandalay,
Fliehen fishlach azoi sheyn,
Der frimorgen kumt vie duner
Fun dem vaser bei Chineh.


## Ver Is Sheyndeleh?

Ver is Sheyndeleh? Vos is zie,
Geloibt bei alleh mentshen?
Gut und frum und sheyn is zie,
Der oilim vil ihr bentshen.
Zieser malach, dos is zie,
Zieser malach, dos is zie.

Gutskeit past ihr vie ah fohn,
Tzadokim tzu ihr gehen;
Ven ah blinder kukt ihr ohn,
Dan ken er veiter zehen;
Und er bleibt dort oiben ohn,
Und er bleibt dort oiben ohn.

Tzu der Sheyndeleh zingen mir,
Zie is ah mentsh an oisnam;
Meiles hot zie ohn ah shir,
Ihr yeder vort hot grois tam.
Blumen krantzen breng ich ihr,
Blumen krantzen breng ich ihr.

# A Red Red Rose

O my love is like a red red rose,
That's newly sprung in June;
O my love is like a melody,
That's sweetly played in tune.

As fair art thou, my bonnie lass,
So deep in love am I;
And I will love thee still, my dear,
Till all the seas go dry.

Till all the seas go dry, my dear,
And the rocks melt with the sun;
And I will love thee still, my dear,
While the sands of life shall run.

And fair thee well, my only love,
And fare thee well a while;
And I will come again, my love,
Though it were ten thousand mile.

ROBERT BURNS

## Ah Roiteh Roz

Mein liebsteh is ah roiteh roz
Vos hot in June geblieht;
Mein liebsteh is ah nigun sheyn
Vos men hot zies geshpielt.

Azoi vie du bist sheyn, mein kind,
Azoi ferliebt bin ich;
Und ich vel zein ferliebt in dir,
Biz yamen trikenen zich.

Der yam vet oisgetrikent zein,
Tzushmoltzen zein der shteyn;
Vie lang ich bin doh af der velt,
Lieb ich nur dir aleyn.

Dan zei gezundt, mein teiereh,
Dos sheiden is beshtelt;
Ich vel tzu dir tzurik kumen,
Afileh fun ek velt.

## The Night Has a Thousand Eyes

The night has a thousand eyes,
And the day but one;
Yet the light of the bright world dies
With the dying sun.

The mind has a thousand eyes,
And the heart but one;
Yet the light of a whole life dies
When love is done.

FRANCIS WILLIAM BOURDILLON

## Die Nacht Hot Toizend Oigen

Die nacht hot toizend oigen,
Der tog hot nur eyns;
Ober dos licht fun der velt geht ois,
Ven die zun fergeht.

Der geist hot toizend oigen,
Dos hartz hot nur eyns;
Ober dos licht fun leben geht ois,
Ven die liebeh shtarbt.

## Swing Low, Sweet Chariot

I looked over Jordan and what did I see,
Coming for to carry me home?
A band of angels coming after me,
Coming for to carry me home.

Swing low sweet chariot,
Coming for to carry me home;
Swing low, sweet chariot,
Coming for to carry me home.

If you get there before I do,
Coming for to carry me home,
Just tell them I'm a-coming too,
Coming for to carry me home.

I aint been to heaven, but I been told,
Coming for to carry me home,
De streets of heaven am paved with gold,
Coming for to carry me home.

I'm sometimes up and sometimes down,
Coming for to carry me home;
But still my soul am heavenly bound,
Coming for to carry me home.

## Nehnter Zich, Liebeh Viegeleh

Ich kuk ibern vasser, und vos zeh ich dort?
Kumen mir tzu fieren aheym—
Ah bandeh malochimlach heilen zich tzu mir—
Zey kumen mir tzu fieren aheym.

Nehnter zich, liebeh viegeleh,
Kum tzu mir und fier mir aheym;
Nehnter zich, du liebeh viegeleh,
Kum tzu mir und fier mir aheym.

Oib ihr vet dort onkumen frieher fun mir,
Oib ihr vet dort kumen aheym;
Zogt zey ohn as ich kum bald tzugehn,
Bald vel ich dort kumen aheym.

In himel bin ich keyn mol nit geven,
Doch hob ich die meiseh gehert—
Die gassen dort zeinen oisgeputzt mit gold—
Vilt zich mir dort kumen aheym.

Amol bin ich freylach, amol ful mit tzar—
Dos leben is mies, oder sheyn;
Doch tzieht die neshomeh dort oiben ohn,
'Svilt zich mir dort kumen aheym.

# Limericks

**1.**

A poet of great reputation,
Who truly deserves adulation;
If only his themes,
Would give life to his dreams—
But no, he is deaf to temptation.

**2.**

A lovely young lass in Decatur,
Devoted she was to her mater;
But her armor was dented,
Her will-power relented,
When a neighbor-lad started to date her.

**3.**

The Mrs. who lives just next door,
Went off to the grocery store;
The glutton's elation,
Proved her ruination—
Now she is my neighbor no more.

**4.**

The world is a mess altogether—
The strife, the pollution, the weather;
How can you avoid it?
We, people, destroyed it—
Let's stay, grin and bear it, together.

ANONYMOUS

## Narishkeiten

**1.**

Ah vichtiker shreiber fun lieder—
Men darf ihm tzukushen die glider;
Ihr hoft zeineh temes,
Erveken dem emes—
Nor dreht zich arum, shreibt er vieder.

**2.**

Ah yunginkeh, sheyninkeh dameh,
Hot eybig gefolgen ihr mameh;
Mit amol vil zie beiten,
Un zein vie bei leiten—
Getrofen ah yungatsh, mistameh.

**3.**

Die veibel vos is mein neksdorkeh,
Avek tzu die grocereh-storkeh;
Zie hot zich fargesen,
Zich gut ongefresen—
Yetst hob ich ah neieh neksdorkeh.

**4.**

Die velt is, in hartzen, ah meser,
Der churben vakst tiefer un greser;
Is vu ken men loifen,
Ah neieh velt koifen?
Doh bleibt men, vet efsher zein beser.

## Home On the Range

Oh give me a home where the buffaloes roam,
Where the deer and the antelope play;
Where seldom is heard a discouraging word,
And the skies are not cloudy all day.

Home, home on the range,
Where the deer and the antelope play;
Where seldom is heard a discouraging word,
And the skies are not cloudy all day.

The air is so pure, and the zephyrs so free,
And the breezes so balmy and light;
That I would not exchange my home on the range,
For all of the cities so bright.

How often at night when the heavens are bright,
With the light from the glittering stars,
Have I stood there amazed, and asked as I gazed,
If their glory exceeds that of ours.

## Irish Eyes

When Irish eyes are smiling,
Sure it's like a day in spring;
In the lilt of Irish laughter,
You can hear the angels sing.

When Irish hearts are happy,
Sure it's like a summer day;
And when Irish eyes are smiling,
Sure they steal your heart away.

## Cowboy Lied

Oi gib mir ah heym vu die bufloksen geyn,
Vu die hirshelach shpielen oif's land;
Keynmol hert men dort ah fertumelten vort,
Un der himel is bloi nochanand.

Heym, dort is mein heym,
Vu die hirshelach shpielen oifs land;
Keyn mol hert men dort ah fertumelten vort,
Un der himel is bloi nochanand.

Die luft is dort rein un die vintelach fein,
Un s'is poshet mechayeh fun Got;
Ich beit keynmol ois, mein land un mein hois,
Far aleh metziehs in shtot.

Vie oftmol beinacht is der himel mit pracht,
Fun die shterner vos glantzen vie gold,
Ich shtey dort entoisht, un in kop meinem roisht,
As die velt is mit vunder betzolt.


## Irisheh Oigen

Ven Irisheh oigen shmeychlen,
Is dos vie ah frilings tog;
In dem Irishen gelechter
Zingt ah zieser malach dort.

Ven Irisheh zeinen freylich,
Is dos sheyn vie zumer teg;
Mit die lachendikeh oigen,
Roiben zey mein hartz avek.

# The Rubaiyat of Omar Khayyam

Wake! For the Sun behind yon Eastern height
Has chased the Session of the Stars from Night;
And, to the field of Heaven ascending, strikes
The sultan's turret with a Shaft of Light.

Before the phantom of False morning died,
Methought a Voice within the Tavern cried,
"When all the Temple is prepared within,
Why lags the drowsy Worshipper outside?"

And, as the Cock crew, those who stood before
The Tavern shouted—"Open then the door!
You know how little while we have to stay,
And, once departed, may return no more."

Come, fill the cup, and in the fire of spring
Your Winter-garment of Repentance fling:
The bird of Time has but a little way
To flutter—and the Bird is on the Wing.

Whether at Naishapur or Babylon,
Whether the Cup with sweet or bitter run,
The Wine of Life keeps oozing drop by drop,
The Leaves of Life keep falling one by one.

Here with a little Bread beneath the Bough,
A Flask of Wine, a Book of Verse—and Thou
Beside me singing in the Wilderness—
Oh, Wilderness were Paradise enow!

Some for the Glories of This World; and some
Sigh for the Prophet's Paradise to come;
Ah, take the cash, and let the promise go,
Nor heed the music of a distant Drum!

## Der Rubaiyat

Vek oif! Die zun fun yenem mizrach-zeit
Hot shoin fertriben aleh shtern fun nacht;
Und vie zie hoibt zich tzu dem himel veit,
Beshtralt zie mit ihr licht dem Sultan's dach.

Eyder der neier morgen is shoin doh,
Ducht mir es ruft ah shtimeh fun dem shenk,
"Der Temple is in gantzen tzugegreyt—
Farvos vartst du in droisen, davener?"

Viebald der huhn hot nor ah kreh getohn,
Dan shreit der oilim, "Effent shoin die tir!
Mir bleiben azah kurtzeh tzeit ot doh—
Und ven men geht, dan kumt men nit tzurik."

Gies ohn dem becher—in dem Friling's feir,
Dos vinter-kleyd, charoteh, varf avek;
Der feygel, Tzeit, hot nur ah kleyneh veg
Tzu flatern; und ot is er shoin nishtoh.

In Naishapur, oder in Babylon—
Der becher zies, oder ah biterer—
Dos vein fun leben rint ois trop noch trop;
Die lebens-bleter falen eyns noch eyns.

Ah lieder-bichel, zitzendik beim boim,
Ah lebel broit, ah fleshel vein, und du—
Du zingst mir tzu—dan vert die vistenish,
An emeser g'n eyden af der velt.

'Sdoh leit vos zuchen glik af unzer velt—
Und and'reh benken noch M'shiach's tzeit—
Nem vos du kenst, genis vos dir gefelt;
Her zich nit ein tzu muzik fun der veit.

Were it not Folly, Spider-like to spin
The Thread of present Life away to win—
What? for ourselves, who know not if we shall
Breathe out the very Breath we now breathe in!

The Worldly Hope men set their Hearts upon
Turns Ashes—or it prospers; and anon,
Like Snow upon the Desert's dusty Face,
Lighting a little hour or two—was gone.

Think, in this battered Caravanserai,
Whose Portals are alternate Night and Day,
How Sultan after Sultan with his Pomp
Abode his destined Hour, and went his way.

Ah, my Beloved, fill the Cup that clears
Today of past Regret and future Fears:
Tomorrow! Why, Tomorrow I may be
Myself with Yesterday's Seven thousand Years.

For some we loved, the loveliest and the best
That from his Vintage rolling Time has prest,
Have drunk their Cup a Round or two before,
And one by one crept silently to rest.

And we, that now make merry in the Room
They left, and Summer dresses in new bloom,
Ourselves must we beneath the Couch of Earth
Descend, ourselves to make a Couch—for whom?

I sometimes think that never blows so red
The Rose as where some buried Caesar bled;
That every Hyacinth the Garden wears
Dropt in her Lap from some once lovely Head.

'Sis narish avekshpinen dem fodim
Fun leben vos is teier und bekant;
Zeinen mir zicher as mir blozen ois
Dem otem vos mir nemen yetzt arein?

Die veltlicheh metziehs vos men zucht,
Oder 'sis ash; oder ah brekil glik,
Vos doiert nur ah kleyneh shtikel tzeit,
Dan shmeltzt es gor avek vie dineh shney.

In der fertzarter Caravanserai,
Vu mir gefinen zich i tog und nacht,
Bemerk vie yeder Sultan in zein shtoltz
Voint zein besherteh shoh, und shtarbt avek.

Geliebteh, gib mir vein vos vasht avek
Fergangeneh charoteh, neieh shrek;
Veil morgen ken ich oich tzuzamen zein
Mit nechtigeh zib'n toizend yohr tzurik.

Gevezen die vos mir hob'n zey gelibt—
Die shensteh und die besteh vos es vaxt;
Zey hoben shoin ferzucht dem lebens-vein,
Dan is zich yeder shtiler-heit avek.

Und mir vos zeinen doh gebliben, und
Vos huliyenen und freyen zich azoi—
Musen mir oichet dort arunter gehn,
Tzu ligen af der shois fun muter erd?

Es ducht zich mir, die roitsteh rozeh vaxt
Dort vu ah Caesar is gefalen toit;
Und as die shensteh veiseh blumeleh
Is die vos hot bedekt an ed'leh kop.

Ah, make the most of what we yet may spend,
Before we too into the Dust descend;
Dust into Dust, and under Dust, to lie,
Sans Wine, sans Song, sans Singer, and—sans End!

Myself when young did eagerly frequent
Doctor and Saint, and heard great argument
About it and about: but evermore
Came out by the same door as in I went.

With them the seed of Wisdom did I sow,
And with my own hand wrought to make it grow:
And this was all the Harvest that I reaped—
"I came like Water, and like Wind I go."

When you and I behind the veil are past,
Oh but the long long while the World shall last,
Which of our coming and Departure heeds
As much as Ocean of a pebble-cast.

Waste not your Hour, nor in the vain pursuit
Of This and That endeavor and dispute;
Better be merry with the fruitful Grape
Than sadden after none, or bitter, Fruit.

Strange, is it not? that of the myriads who
Before us passed the door of Darkness through,
Not one returns to tell us of the Road,
Which to discover we must travel too.

The Moving Finger writes; and, having writ,
Moves on: nor all your piety nor Wit
Shall lure it back to cancel half a Line,
Nor all your Tears wash out a Word of it.

Genis alts vos du kenst, as du host tzeit,
Eder fun uns vet oichet veren shtoib;
Shtoib geht tzu shtoib, und unter shtoib tzu zein—
Ohn vein, ohn lied, ohn zinger, und ohn sof.

Als yungerman, fleg ich zehr oft dor gehn
Tzum lerer und tzum tzadik, einshepen
Erklerungen, und tiefeh meinungen—
Und 'chbin arois der zelber vie arein.

Mit zey tzuzamen hob ich eingeflantzt
Dos kerendel fun chochmeh; hob's bedient.
Mein gantzeh ernteh is: "Vie vaser bin
Ich doh gekumen; und ich geh vie vint."

Ven du und ich zeinen shoin mehr nitoh,
Die velt vet doieren ah langeh tzeit;
Tzu gehen mir, tzu kumen, art es ihr
Punkt vie der yam bemerkt ah shteyndeleh.

Ferdarbeh nit dein shtundeh—'sis umzist
Tzu shtreiten ieber yedeh mindsteh zach;
Besser anoyeh hoben fun dem vein,
Eyder fun biterkeit umgliklich zein.

'Sis modneh—fun die fieleh toizenter
Vos zeinen duch die Finstereh Tir arois,
Kumt keyner nit tzurik mohlen dem veg—
Mir musen oisgefinen dos aleyn.

Der Finger shreibt—und rirt zich noch-a-nand—
Dein frumkeit, dein fershtandt, und deineh trer'n,
Kenen nit poilen er zol oismeken
Ah halbeh shureh, oder chotsch eyn vort.

And that inverted Bowl we call The Sky,
Whereunder crawling cooped we live and die,
Lift not your hands to IT for help—for It
As impotently rolls as you or I.

Oh Thou, who Man of baser Earth didst make,
And ev'n with Paradise devise the Snake:
For all the Sin the Face of wretched Man
Is black with—Man's Forgiveness give—and take!

And much as Wine has played the Infidel,
And robbed me of my Robe of Honor—Well,
I often wonder what the Vintners buy
One-half so precious as the ware they sell.

Yet Ah, that Spring should vanish with the Rose!
That Youth's sweet-scented manuscript should close!
The Nightingale that in the branches sang,
Ah whence, and whither flown again, who knows?

Ah Love! could you and I with Fate conspire
To grasp this sorry Scheme of Things entire,
Would not we shatter it to bits—and then
Re-mould it nearer to the Heart's Desire!

But see! The rising Moon of Heaven again
Looks for us, Sweetheart, through the quivering Plane:
How oft hereafter rising will she look
Among those leaves—for one of us in vain!

And when Yourself with silver Foot shall pass
Among the Guests Star-scattered on the Grass,
And in your joyous errand reach the spot
Where I made One—turn down an empty Glass!

OMAR KHAYYAM

Dos umgekerteh shisel—der himel
Vos unter ihm mir krichen bis dem toit—
Heyb nit die hendt, und bet ihm nit far hilf,
Veil er is azoi shvach vie du und ich.

O Du, vos host dem mentsh gemacht fun erd,
Und in g'n eyden host bezetst die shlang—
Far alleh die aveyrehs der mentsh leidt,
Gib ihm fergebens, Got, und nem oich zein.

Afileh as der vein hot mir benart,
Und hot beroibt dem kovid vos mir kumt—
Vos kenen vein-hendler far zich koifen,
Vos is azoi min teier vie der vein?

Farvos fergeht der Friling mit die rozeh?
Farvos, tzu zieser yugend, gibts ah sof?
Vu is die nachtigal ferfloigen den,
Vos hot gezungen in dem boim—ver veys?

Oi teiereh! oib du und ich volten
Gekent die shlechteh velt ibermachen,
Mir volten es af pitzelach tzuhakt,
Und dan geboit ah neieh, besereh.

Zeh nor vie die levoneh heybt zich oif—
Zie zucht uns durch die bletter, teiereh;
Vie oft vet zie amol zuchen umzist,
Veil eyner fun uns vet shoin mehr nit zein.

Ven du mit leichten fissel geyst arum
Tzvishen die gest ferbreitert af die groz,
Und in dein lieben gang kumst tzu dem platz
Vu ich fleg zein—ferker ah pusteh gloz.

## Nursery Rhyme

Baa baa black sheep,
Have you any wool?
Yes sir, yes sir,
Three bags full.

One for my master,
One for his dame,
One for the little boy,
Who lives down the lane.

Baa baa black sheep,
Have you any wool?
Yes sir, yes sir,
Three bags full.

## America

My country 'tis of thee,
Sweet land of liberty,
Of thee I sing;
Land where my fathers died,
Land of the Pilgrims' pride,
From every mountain side,
Let freedom ring.

Our fathers' God, to Thee,
Author of liberty,
To Thee we sing;
Long may our land be bright,
With freedom's holy light,
Protect us by Thy might,
Great God our king.

## Kinder-Shpiel

Ba ba shefeleh,
Efsher hostu vul?
Vos far ah frageh—
Drei torbehs ful.

Eyns far dem balebos,
Eyns far zein veib;
Eyns far dem yingeleh,
Tzudeken zein leib.

Ba ba shefeleh,
Efsher hostu vul?
Freg nit keyn kashes,
Nem zich torbehs ful.


## Amerika

Mein land, mit guts gekroint,
Vu zieseh freiheit voint,
Fun dir ich zing;
Land fun die Pilgrim's tzeit,
Mein folk hot dort geleit,
Berger af yeder zeit,
Mit freiheit kling.

Foter fun unzer velt,
Freiheit host du beshtelt,
Ich zing tzu dir;
Frei zol zein unzer land,
Eybig, und noch-a-nand
Behit uns, mit dein hand—
Dos beten mir.

[75]

## Selections from Emily Dickinson

**1.**

I never saw a moor,
I never saw the sea;
Yet know I how the heather looks,
And what a wave must be.

I never spoke with God,
Nor visited in heaven;
Yet certain am I of the spot,
As if the chart were given.

**2.**

If I can stop one heart from breaking,
I shall not live in vain;
If I can ease one life the aching,
Or cool one pain;
Or help one fainting robin
Into his nest again,
I shall not live in vain.

## Fun Emily Dickinson

**1.**

'Chob nit gezehn ah stepp,
Keynmol gezehn dem yam;
Doch veys ich vie 'skukt ois dos groz,
Und vos ah chvalieh is.

'Chob nit geredt mit Got,
Und nit bezucht in himel;
Doch bin ich zicher 'chken dem platz
Vie 'chvolt ah karteh hoben.

**2.**

Oib ich ken machen eyn hartz gringer,
Dan leb ich nit umzist;
Oib ich mach vemens tzorehs leichter,
Und tzu derleiden—
Chotsh helfen eyn kleyn feygeleh
Tzurik in nest arein—
Dan leb ich nit umzist.

Four score and seven years ago our fathers brought forth on this continent a new nation, conceived in liberty and dedicated to the proposition that all men are created equal.

Now we are engaged in a great civil war, testing whether that nation or any nation so conceived and so dedicated, can long endure. We are met on a great battlefield of that war. We have come to dedicate a portion of that field, as a final resting place for those who here gave their lives that that nation might live. It is altogether fitting and proper that we do this.

But in a larger sense, we cannot dedicate—we cannot consecrate—we cannot hallow this ground. The brave men, living and dead, who struggled here, have consecrated it, far above our poor power to add or detract. The world will little note, nor long remember, what we say here, but it can never forget what they did here. It is for us the living, rather, to be dedicated here to the great task remaining before us—that from these honored dead we take increased devotion to that cause for which they gave the last full measure of devotion. That we here highly resolve that these dead shall not have died in vain—that this nation, under God, shall have a new birth of freedom—and that government of the people, by the people, for the people, shall not perish from the earth.

*November 19, 1863*

## Lincoln's Gettysburg Redeh

Zieben-und-achtzig yohr tzurik, hoben unzereh elteren beshtelt af diesen velt-teil ah neien folk, begreift in freiheit, und
gevidmet tzu die forshlageh as alleh mentshen zeinen beshafen
gleich.

Yetzt fieren mir ohn ah shveren birger-krig, tzu prubiren
oib dieser folk, oder velcher es is folk, vos is azoi begreift und
azoi gevidmet, ken lang doieren. Mir treffen zich doh af ah
groissen melchomeh-feld fun diesen krig. Mir zeinen zich tzuzamen gekumen tzu vidmen ah teil fun dem feld als ah beys-
oilim far die neshomes vos hoben geshonken zeyer leben as der
folk zol oishalten. Es is zehr richtig, es past zich, as mir zolen
dos tohn.

Ober fun ah gresseren shtandpunkt, kennen mir nit vidmen,
mir kenen nit beheiligen, mir kennen nit m'kadish zein diesen
ort. Die helden vos hoben doh gekemft—die vos leben, und
die vos zeinen geshtorben—zey hoben shoin dem ort heilig gemacht. Unzereh oremeh koiches kennen datzu gornit tzulegen.
Die gantzeh velt vet kam bemerken vos mir zogen doh; ober
zie vet keynmol nit fergessen vos zey hoben doh oisgefirt. Mir,
die lebedigeh, mussen zich doh tzushveren as mir velen endigen
die arbet vos zey, die kriger, hoben azoi edel ongefangen. Es is
besser as mir zolen zich doh vidmen tzu die groiseh oifgabeh
vos bleibt doh—as fun diezeh beerteh neshomes vet uns tzukum-
en ah gresserer chayshik oistzufiren die oifgabeh, far velcheh
zey hoben tzugelegt mit zeyer leben. Mir mussen doh beshliesen
as unzereh toiteh zeinen nit geshtorben umzist—und as unzer
folk, mit Got's hilf, vet nochamol zein frei. Und as die regirung
fun die mentshen, bei die mentshen, und far die mentshen, zol
nit umkumen fun der velt.

# The New Colossus

Not like the brazen giant of Greek fame,
With conquering limbs astride from land to land;
Here at our sea-washed, sunset gates shall stand
A mighty woman with a torch, whose flame
Is the imprisoned lightning, and her name
Mother of Exiles. From her beacon-hand
Glows world-wide welcome; her mild eyes command
The air-bridged harbor that twin cities frame.
"Keep, ancient lands, your storied pomp!" cries she
With silent lips. "Give me your tired, your poor,
Your huddled masses yearning to breathe free,
The wretched refuse of your teeming shore.
Send these, the homeless, tempest-tossed to me,
I lift my lamp beside the golden door!"

EMMA LAZARUS

## Der Neier Kolosus

Nit vie der riz fun kuper, fun die Grichen,
Mit zeineh fis vos shpanen land tzu land;
Doh beim toier leben vaser, vet shtehn
Ah vunder-froi, mit ah shturkaz in hant,
Fun dem vet flamen der farshparter blitz.
Zie heyst Muter fun die Fertribeneh,
Un zie begrist die voglers mit ihr flam;
Mit shtileh lipen zogt zie ihr besureh—
"Halt zich mit eier pompes, alteh lender;
Git mir die miedeh, un die oremeh,
Un die dershrokeneh vos benken tzu zein frei,
Alleh umgliklicheh, der oisvurf fun dein land.
Shikt die farfolgteh, heymlozeh, tzu mir;
Ich halt mein lomp hoich, bei der goldn'r tir."

# SONNETS

How do I love thee? Let me count the ways.
I love thee to the depth and breadth and height
My soul can reach, when feeling out of sight
For the ends of Being and ideal Grace.
I love thee to the level of every day's
Most quiet need, by sun and candlelight.
I love thee freely, as men strive for Right;
I love thee purely, as they turn from Praise.
I love thee with the passion put to use
In my old griefs, and with my childhood's faith.
I love thee with a love I seemed to lose
With my lost saints—I love thee with the breath,
Smiles, tears, of all my life! and if God choose,
I shall but love thee better after death.

ELIZABETH BARRETT BROWNING


I cry you mercy—pity—love! aye, love!
Merciful love that tantalizes not.
One-thoughted, never-wandering, guileless love,
Unmasked, and being seen—without a blot!
O! let me have thee whole—all, all be mine!
That shape, that fairness, that sweet minor zest
Of love, your kiss, Those hands, those eyes divine,
That warm, white, lucent, million-pleasured breast,
Yourself—your soul—in pity give me all,
Withhold no atom's atom, or I die;
Or living on perhaps, your wretched thrall,
Forget, in the mist of idle misery,
Life's purposes—the palate of my mind
Losing its gust, and my ambition blind!

JOHN KEATS

[84]

Vifiel hob ich dir lieb? Loz mir tzelen:
Ich lieb dir azoi tief und breit und hoich
Vie mein neshomeh ken dergreichen, ven
Zie zucht dem lebens tachlis und die shchineh.
Ich lieb dir vie men zucht ah shtilleh shoh
Vens endikt zich ah moirediker tog.
Mit fullen villen, vie men zucht dos Rechts;
Mit fullen hartzen, vie men hast dos shlechts.
Ich lieb dir mit ah feier vos brent fun tzorehs,
Und mit der angst fun kindheit vos zucht ruh.
Ich lieb dir azoi shtark vie svilt zich gloiben
As es gefinen zich tzadokim af der velt.
Ich lieb dir fun mein leben's tiefsten noit—
Und, oib Got lozt, vel ich dir lieben nochn toit.


Ich bet dir mitleid, liebeh, und rachmonehs.
Liebeh vos kvelt nit durch getoishteh hofnung;
Eyn-hartzig, ehrlich, und getreieh liebeh,
Vie men derkent es—liebeh ohn ah shoten.
Ich vil dir hoben—zolst zein mein aleyn;
Dein zis geshtalt, dein sheynkeit, dein geshmak
Fun liebeh, dein kush; die hentelach,
Die sheyneh oigen, und die veiseh brust.
Dein gantzer vezen, dein neshomeh—
Ich bet dir—gib mir alts, alts zol zein mein—
Halt nit tzurik, anit shtarb ich avek;
Und oib ich leben bleib, bin ich dein shklaf.
Dan bin ich elend—ohn tachlis, ohn fershtand—
Und vie ah blinder, zuch ich nochanand.

Were I as base as is the lowly plain,
And you, my Love, as high as heaven above,
Yet should the thoughts of me, your humble swain,
Ascend to heaven in honor of my love.
Were I as high as heaven above the plain,
And you, my Love, as humble and as low
As are the deepest bottoms of the main,
Wheresoe'er you were, with you my love should go.
Were you the earth, dear Love, and I the skies,
My love should shine on you like to the sun,
And look upon you with ten thousand eyes,
Till heaven waxed blind, and till the world were done.
Wheresoe'er I am—below, or else above you—
Wheresoe'er you are, my heart shall truly love you.

JOSHUA SYLVESTER


More than most fair, full of the living fire
Kindled above, unto the Maker near;
No eyes, but joys, in which all powers conspire,
That to the world naught else be counted dear:
Through your bright beams doth not the blinded guest
Shoot out his darts to base affection's wound,
But angels come, to lead frail minds to rest,
In chaste desires, on heavenly beauty bound.
You frame my thoughts, and fashion me within
You stop my tongue, and teach my heart to speak,
You calm the storm that passion did begin,
Strong though your cause, but by your virtue weak.
Dark is the world where your light shined never;
Well is he born that may behold you ever.

EDMUND SPENSER

Ven ich bin niederig vie die flacheh erd,
Und du, mein shatz, bist vie der himel hoich—
Meineh gedanken, chotsh ich bin gemein,
Aruf tzu dir, geliebteh, fliehen zey.
Nor tomer bin ich hoich iber der erd,
Und du, mein teiereh, bist afen grund,
Azoi min tief, as tiefer ken nit zein—
Mein hartz volt dir gefunen umetum.
Bist du die erd, und ich der himel bloi,
Mein liebeh volt dir sheinen vie die zun;
Mit toizend oigen kuk ich nor af dir,
Vie lang 'sis doh ah himel und ah velt.
Vu nor ich bin—tzu niederig, tzu grois,
Vu nor du bist, mein hartz gefint dir ois.


Shener bist du vie alleh andereh;
Brenst mit ah flam vos Got hot ongetzunden;
Die oigen deineh—azah freyd, ah macht
Vos zogt der velt, beser is nit gefunden.
Durch deineh shtrahlen, der ferblinter gast
Zucht tzu dergreichen deineh tiefsteh liebeh;
Shtilen zein leidenshaft und heysen feier,
Kumen malochimlach, dich obtzuhiten.
Du gibst ah grois geshtalt tzu mein gedanken;
Mein tzung vert shtum, mein hartz vil tzu dir reden;
Und du beruhigst mein tzuflamteh liebeh—
Dein gutskeit macht mir shtark, veil du fershemst mir.
Die velt is finster, vu men bleibt ohn dir;
Und gliklich is der, vos is nohnt tzu dir.

Remember me when I am gone away,
Gone far away into the silent land;
When you can no more hold me by the hand,
Nor I half turn to go, yet turning stay.
Remember me when no more, day by day,
You tell me of our future that you planned;
Only remember me; you understand
It will be late to counsel then or pray.
Yet if you should forget me for a while
And afterwards remember, do not grieve;
For if the darkness and corruption leave
A vestige of the thoughts that once I had,
Better by far you should forget and smile,
Than that you should remember and be sad.

CHRISTINA ROSSETTI



When you and I have played the little hour,
Have seen the tall subaltern Life to Death
Yield up his sword; and, smiling, draw the breath,
The first long breath of freedom; when the flower
Of Recompense hath fluttered to our feet,
As to an actor's; and, the curtain down,
We turn to face each other all alone—
Alone, we two, who never yet did meet,
Alone, and absolute, and free: O then,
O then most dear, how shall be told the tale?
Clasped hands, pressed lips, and so clasped hands again;
No words. But as the proud wind fills the sail,
My love to yours shall reach, then one deep moan
Of joy, and then our infinite Alone.

GILBERT PARKER

Gedenk mir ven ich bin shoin mehr nitto—
Avek in yener veiter, shtiller land;
Ven du kenst mir nit halten bei der hant,
Ich fleg zich greyten gehn, und bleiben shtehn.
Gedenk mir ven du kenst nit, vie amol,
Teglich ah plan fun unzer tzukunft veben;
Gedenk, afileh as 'svet zein tzu shpeht
Tzu hofen, oder zich ahn eytzeh geben.
Nur oib du vest fergesen vegen mir,
Und shpeter zich dermonen, zorg zich nit;
Veil oib die shvereh finsternish fun toit
Lozt iber chotsh ah shpur fun yeneh teg—
Is beser zolst fergesen und zein frei,
Eyder gedenken und fertroiert zein.

Ven du und ich hoben fershpielt die shoh—
Hoben gezehn vie leben fiert tzum toit;
Ven mir hoben fershtanen as dos is
Die emeseh befreiheit fun dos noit;
Ven die beloinung falt tzu unz'reh fies,
Vie blumen flateren tzu dem aktior—
Bleiben mir shtehn tzuzamen, gantz aleyn—
Aleyn zeinen mir yetzt, tzum ershten mol;
Aleyn, ferzichert, shtoltz, und emes frei.
Anu mein teiereh, vos vet zein yetzt?
Die hent tzuzamen, und die lipen oich—
Verter zeinen umzist. Vie zeglen ful mit vint,
Shtrekt zich mein liebeh ois tzu dir, ah zifts
Fun freyd—und dan der eybiger Aleyn.

Fly to her heart, hover about her heart,
With dainty kisses mollify her heart,
Pierce with thy arrows her obdurate heart,
With sweet allurements ever move her heart.
At mid-day and at midnight touch her heart,
Be lurking closely, nestle about her heart,
With power (thou art a god), command her heart,
Kindle thy coals of love about her heart,
Yea, even into thyself transform her heart.
Ah, she must love! Be sure thou have her heart,
And I must die if thou have not her heart.
Thy bed, if thou rest well, must be her heart,
He hath the best part sure, that hath her heart.
What have I not, if I have but her heart!

BARTHOLOMEW GRIFFIN


I send you here a wreath of blossoms blown,
And woven flowers at sunset gathered;
Another dawn had seen them ruined, and shed
Loose leaves upon the grass at random strown.
By this, their sure example, be it known,
That all your beauties, now in perfect flower,
Shall fade as these, and wither in an hour.
Flowerlike, and brief of days, as the flower sown.
Ah, time is flying, lady—time is flying;
Nay, 'tis not time that flies, but we that go,
Who in short space shall be in churchyard lying,
And of our loving parley none shall know,
Nor any man consider what we were.
Be therefore kind, my love, whilst thou art fair.

PIERRE DE RONSARD

Flieh tzu ihr hartz, flater arum ihr hartz,
Mit leichteh kushen shmeltz avek ihr hartz;
Mit deinen boigen shtech ihr akshen-hartz,
Mit zieseh reyd nehnter zich tzu ihr hartz.
Bei tog und oich bei nacht rir ohn ihr hartz,
Praveh zich shtendig dort arum ihr hartz;
Bist doch ah Got, mit macht befehl ihr hartz,
Tzind on dem koil fun liebeh in ihr hartz.
Afileh nehm arein in zich, ihr hartz.
Zie mus lieben! zolst tzunemen ihr hartz,
Anit shtarb ich, oib du host nit ihr hartz.
Vilst du gut ruhen, is dein bet ihr hartz.
Er hot dos besteh, ver es hot ihr hartz;
Vos felt mir ois, abi ich hob ihr hartz.




Ich shik tzu dir ah sheynem blumenkrantz—
Gezamelt hob ich blumelach in ovent;
Af morgen volt shoin zein ah tel fun zey—
Die bletlach afen groz tzushoten.
Fun diezen beishpiel, ken ah mentsh fershtehn,
Die gresteh sheynheit, vie ah feineh blum,
Vet zein fervelkt, ferdorben, in ah shoh;
Punkt vie ah tzarteh blum vet zie fergehn.
Oi, teiereh, die tzeit flieht shnel ferbei—
Azoi velen mir aleh shnel avek;
Und ven mir in dem kalten keyver liegen,
Vet keyner nit gedenken unzer liebeh.
Keyner vet unzer leidenshaft fershtehn—
Toh zei mir gut, mein shatz, vie lang bist sheyn.

When I have fears that I may cease to be
Before my pen has gleaned my teeming brain,
Before high-piled books, in charactry,
Hold like full garners the full-ripened grain;
When I behold, upon the night's starred face,
Huge cloudy symbols of a high romance,
And feel that I may never live to trace
Their shadows, with the magic hand of chance;
And when I feel, fair creature of an hour!
That I shall never look upon thee more,
Never have relish in the faery power
Of unreflecting love;—then on the shore
Of the wide world I stand alone, and think,
Till Love and Fame to nothingness do sink.

JOHN KEATS


My true love hath my heart and I have his,
By just exchange one for the other given.
I hold his dear, and mine he cannot miss,
There never was a better bargain driven.
His heart in me keeps me and him in one;
My heart in him his thoughts and senses guides;
He loves my heart, for once it was his own;
I cherish his, because in me it bides.
His heart his wound received from my sight;
My heart was wounded with his wounded heart;
For as from me on him his hurt did light,
So still methought in me his hurt did smart;
Both equal hurt, in this change sought our bliss
My true love hath my heart, and I have his.

SIR PHILIP SIDNEY

Ven ich nem zorgen as ich shtarb avek,
Eyder mein feder hot gezamelt dort
Vos ligt bei mir in kop; die fieleh bicher
Vos ich vil shreiben fun mein fruchtbarkeit;
Ven ich kuk af die shterner fun der nacht,
Und zeh ah tseichen fun ah grois roman—
Dan hob ich moireh ich vel nit derleben
Bekant veren mit dem berimten tam;
Ven ich derzeh vie sheyn du bist, und tracht
As bald vest du af eybig fun mir gehn;
Dein zieseh liebeh hob ich nit genisen,
Dein sheynem ponim vel ich mehr nit zehn.
Dan bleib ich gantz aleyn, und bei zich tracht—
As alts is gornisht, alts vert umgebracht.


Mein liebster hot mein hartz, und ich hob zeins—
Dos hoben mir zich ehrlich oisgebiten;
Ich shetz zein hartz; bei ihm is mein hartz teier—
Ah bes'ren handel, ken men nit begreifen.
Zein hartz bei mir, bleiben mir vie eyn mentsh;
Mein hartz bei ihm, veizst ihm dem guten veg;
Er liebt mein hartz, veil 'shot gehert tzu ihm;
Ich ehreh zeins, veil yetzt voint es bei mir.
Mein blik af ihm, hot ihm zein hartz fervundet;
Zein vund, hot mir mein hartz tzutreyselt;
Azoi vie ich hob ihm zein hartz tzurisen,
Azoi macht er mein heyseh treren fliesen.
Beydeh fervundet, beydeh shtark ferliebt—
Er hot mein hartz, und zein hartz bei mir ligt.

For certain he hath seen all perfectness
Who among other ladies hath seen mine:
They that go with her humbly should combine
To thank their God for such peculiar grace.
So perfect is the beauty of her face
That it begets in no wise any sign
Of envy, but draws round her a clear line
Of love, and blessed faith, and gentleness.
Merely the sight of her makes all things bow;
Not she herself is holier
Than all; but hers, through her, are raised above.
From all her acts such lovely graces flow.
That truly one may never think of her
Without a passion of exceeding love.

DANTE ALIGHIERI


When men shall find thy flower, thy glory, pass,
And thou, with careful brow sitting alone,
Received hast this message from thy glass,
That tells the truth and says that all is gone:
Fresh shalt thou see in me the wounds thou madest,
Though spent by flame, in me the heat remaining;
I that have loved thee thus before thou fadest,
My faith shall wax when thou art in thy waning.
The world shall find this miracle in me,
That fire can burn then all the matter's spent;
Then what my faith hath been, thyself shall see,
And that thou wast unkind, thou mayest repent.
Thou mayest repent that thou hast scorned my tears,
When winter snows upon thy sable hairs.

SAMUEL DANIEL

Der vos af mein gelibteh hot gekukt,
Er hot gezehn dos besteh vos es gibt;
Und die vos kenen ihr, zey danken Got,
Veil er hot zey ihr herlichkeit geshikt.
Azoi betamt is zie, und azoi sheyn!
Ver mit ihr cheyn und gutskeit is bekent,
Der is gebentsht; er fielt zich vie beneit;
Zein hartz vert ful mit liebeh und mit freyd
Eyn blik af ihr, und shchineh falt arop,
Ah tfileh af die lipen; zie is tzart,
Und zie is heylig; die vos zeinen nohnt,
Veren begeistert fun ihr gegenvart.
Zie is ah malach, tzu der erd fertriebt—
As men betracht ihr, is men bald ferliebt.


'Svet zein ah tog, dein sheynheit vet fergehn,
Und du, beim shpiegel zitsendig aleyn,
Begreifst dem emes, vie er veist dir ohn—
Shoin mer nitto die yugend, und dos cheyn.
Dan vest du zehn in mir die alteh vunden,
Der flam ferloshen, die varemkeit noch doh;
Ich fleg dir lieben ven du bist geven yinger,
Yetst af der elter, gloib ich alts in dir.
Die velt vet zehn in mir a groisen vunder—
As feier ken brenen, vens nitto mit vos;
Und dan vest du fershtehn mein amuneh,
Und vest charoteh hoben far dein groizamkeit
Du vest bereien meineh heyseh treren,
Ven deineh shvartzeh loken veiseh veren.

Since there's no help, come let us kiss and part;
Nay, I have done, you get no more of me;
And I am glad, yea, glad with all my heart,
That thus so cleanly I myself can free.
Shake hands for ever, cancel all our vows,
And, when we meet at any time again,
Be it not seen in either of our brows
That we one jot of former love retain.
Now at the last gasp of love's latest breath,
When, his pulse failing, Passion speechless lies,
When Faith is kneeling by his bed of death,
And Innocence is closing up his eyes—
Now if thou wouldst, when all have given him over,
From death to life thou might'st him yet recover.

MICHAEL DRAYTON

Stubborn and proud, I carry my head high;
Haughty by birth, inflexible by mood,
I would not bow to any king; I would
Not even veil my candid gaze, not I.
But, mother, never let me dare deny
How soon my pride, my boastful hardihood
Shamed by your presence and solicitude,
Leaves me without one small departing sigh.
Is it your spirit that o'ermasters me,
Your lofty, penetrating soul that clears
The earth and cleaves to heaven, flying free?
Memory burns and rankles, for I know
How often I have brought your heart to tears,
The soft and suffering heart that loved me so.

HEINRICH HEINE

Ferfalen—gib mir ah kush, lomir zich sheiden;
'Smuz zein ah sof, mehr maters du mir nit;
Ich bin tzufrieden, fun mein tiefsten hartzen,
Dos azoi grindlich ken ich zich befreien.
Gib mir dein hant, zol yeder gehn zein veg;
Oismeken mir aleh fershprechungen;
Und oib mir trefen zich amol, vu ergetz,
Zol men fun liebeh nit ah simen zehn.
Yetzt, ven die liebeh halt shoin lang bei shtarben,
Ven leidenshaft is oisgevebt und shvach;
Ven treiheit kniet zich, shtark ferzorgt, fertzveifelt,
Und umshuld, macht die troirig oigen tzu—
Yetzt, oib du vilst, oib host die liebeh gern,
Fun toit tzum leben kenst du ihm umkeren.

Shtoltz bin ich, eingeshpart, halt hoich die kop;
Geboiren mazeldik, vil zich nit boigen;
Tzu keynem neyg ah kni—nit tzu ah kenig,
Und ich kuk alemen gleich in die oigen.
Ober, mein muter, ich ken nit ferneigen
As mein shtoltzieren und berimerei,
Veren ferloren, in gantzen oisgemekt,
Vibald du kumst doh mit dein edelkeit.
Is dos dein geist vos ibermechtigt mir,
Dein forshendeh neshomeh, vos hoibt zich
Iber erd, und nehntert zich tzum himel?
Die erinerung erbitert mir, veil
Ich veys vie oft 'chob ful gemacht mit treren
Dein veycheh hartz, vos hot mir azoi gern.

Shall I compare thee to a summer's day?
Thou art more lovely and more temperate.
Rough winds do shake the darling buds of May,
And summer's lease hath all too short a date:
Sometimes too hot the eye of heaven shines,
And often is his gold complexion dimmed:
And every fair from fair sometime declines,
By chance, or nature's changing course, untrimmed:
But thy eternal summer shall not fade,
Nor lose possession of that fair thou owest;
Nor shall Death brag thou wanderest in his shade,
When in eternal lines to time thou growest.
So long as men can breathe, or eyes can see,
So long lives this, and this gives life to thee.

WILLIAM SHAKESPEARE


Your hands lie open in the long fresh grass,
The finger-points look through like rosy blooms;
Your eyes smile peace. The pasture gleams and glooms
Neath billowing skies that scatter and amass.
All round our nest, far as the eye can pass,
Are golden kingcup fields with silver edge,
Where the cow-parsley skirts the hawthorn-hedge.
'Tis visible silence, still as the hour-glass.
Deep in the sun-searched growths the dragon-fly
Hangs like a blue thread loosened from the sky:
So this winged hour is dropt to us from above.
Oh! clasp we to our hearts, for deathless dower,
This close-companioned inarticulate hour,
When two-fold silence was the song of love.

DANTE GABRIEL ROSSETTI

Zol ich dir gleichen tzu a zumer tog?
Neyn, du bist shener; milder is dein mut.
Vinten tzureisen blumelach in Mai;
Und zieser zumer loift tzu shnel farbei.
Faranen teg ven's brent tzu shtark die zun;
Und and'reh teg, zeht men ihm gornit ohn;
Afileh sheynkeit vert amol fervelkt—
Men ken zich nit ferlozen af natur.
Ober dein zumer eybig bleibht, und frish;
Dein sheynkeit, zie vet keynmol nit fergehn;
Der mlach-hamovehs vet zich nit berimen,
As du, in zein medineh, bist gekumen.
Vie lang 'svet zein ahn oilim vos ken lezen,
In diezeh shurehs bleibst du imer leben.




Die hent deineh, liegen ofen in groz,
Die fingerlach vie roiteh blumelach;
Die oigen shmeychlen mit ah zieseh ruh—
Unter dem himel finkelt sheyn die pasheh.
Arum uns, azoi veit vie oigen zehn,
Shpreyten zich felder mit ah golden weitz;
Und veiseh petrushkeh vaxt dort arumet—
Die shtilkeit is azoinst, men ken es zehen.
Tief in die zunig ritlach hengt ah flieg,
Punkt vie ah bloier fodim hengt es dort;
Azoi shnel is die shtundeh uns geshonken.
Lomir fest ohnemen tzu unzereh hertzer,
Die unshterblicheh shtundeh—ah matoneh—
Die shtilkeit, ah gezang fun unzer liebeh.

It is a beauteous evening, calm and free;
The holy time is quiet as a nun
Breathless with adoration; the broad sun
Is sinking down in its tranquility;
The gentleness of heaven broods o'er the sea;
Listen! the mighty Being is awake,
And doth with his eternal motion make
A sound like thunder—everlastingly.
Dear child! dear girl! that walkest with me here,
If thou appear untouched by solemn thought,
Thy nature is not therefore less divine:
Thou liest in Abraham's bosom all the year,
And worshipst at the Temple's inner shrine,
God being with thee when we know it not.

WILLIAM WORDSWORTH


Ah, were she pitiful as she is fair,
Or but as mild as she is seeming so,
Then were my hopes greater than my despair,
Then all the world were heaven, nothing woe.
Ah, were her heart relenting as her hand,
That seems to melt even with the mildest touch,
Then knew I where to seat me in a land
Under wide heavens, but yet there is none such.
So, as she shows, she seems the budding rose,
Yet sweeter far than is an earthly flower;
Sovran of beauty! like the spray she grows,
Compassed she is with thorns and cankered bower.
Yet were she willing to be plucked and worn,
She would be gathered, though she grew on thorn.

ROBERT GREENE

Es is ah sheyner ovent, ruhig, frei;
Die tzeit ven es is shtil—vie ah monashkeh
Fertieft in ihreh heylikeh tefilehs;
Die breiteh zun fergeht in ruhigkeit.
Der himel hengt fertracht iber dem yam;
Her zich nur ein—der vasser shloft nit;
Zein voien und zein eybiger bevegung,
Dunert nochanand, und ohn ah sof.
Teiereh meydel, du shpatzierst mit mir,
Bist nit bezitst mit vichtikeh gedanken;
Doch die neshomeh deineh heylig is;
Du tuliest zich tzu getlichkeit ah gantzen yohr,
In tiefsten hartzen du bedienst dein Got—
Der Oibershter bevacht dir imer.

Ven zie hot mitleid, azoi vie zie's sheyn,
Und tzertlichkeit, vie 'sducht zich as zie hot—
Dan volt ich hofen, nit fertzveifelt zein;
Dan is mein velt g'neyden—vie bei Got.
Ven zie volt zein barmhertzig, vie ihr hant
Vos vert tzushmoltzen, ven ich rir es ohn—
Dan volt ich visen as ich hob ah land
Mit bloieh himlen—nor es is nittoh.
Es ducht zich as zie is ah zieseh roz—
Fiel shener vie die blumen af der velt;
Groisartig zie—doch vaxt zie vie ah tzveig,
Arumringelt mit dornen, und mit kelt.
Doch, oib zie volt mir lozen, volt ich gern
Ihr kleiben tzu zich—fun ah dorn, ah shtern.

Set me whereas the sun doth parch the green,
Or where his beams do not dissolve the ice;
In temperate heat, where he is felt and seen;
In presence prest of people mad or wise;
Set me in high, or yet in low degree;
In longest night, or in the shortest day;
In clearest sky, or where clouds thickest be;
In lusty youth, or when my hairs are grey.
Set me in heaven, in earth, or else in hell,
In hill or dale, or in the foaming flood;
Thrall, or at large, alive whereso I dwell,
Sick or in health, in evil fame or good.
Hers will I be; and only with this thought
Content myself, although my chance be nought.

FRANCESCO PETRARCA


When in disgrace with fortune and men's eyes,
I all alone beweep my outcast state,
And trouble deaf heaven with my bootless cries,
And look upon myself, and curse my fate;
Wishing me like to one more rich in hope,
Featured like him, like him with friends possessed;
Desiring this man's art, and that man's scope,
With what I most enjoy contented least;
Yet in these thoughts myself almost despising.
Haply I think on thee—and then my state,
Like to the lark at break of day arising
From sullen earth, sings hymns at heaven's gate;
For thy sweet love remembered such wealth brings,
That then I scorn to change my state with kings.

WILLIAM SHAKESPEARE

Shtel mir avek dort vu es brent die zun,
Oder dort vu 'sis shtendig eis und kalt;
In mildeh klimat, vu 'sis angenehm,
Tzu vu es is ahn oilim; ah gevalt.
Mach mir zein shtoltz, tzu mach fun mir ah tel—
In langeh nacht, oder in kurtzen tog;
Vu 'sis der himel klor, tzu volkendig—
In yugend, oder ven ich bin shoin groi.
Af erd, g'neyden, oder gor in drerd—
Af berg, in tol, in vaser ven es fliest;
Ah shklaf, tzu frei, vu 'sken nit zein ich voin,
Gezundt, tzu krank; bin ich berimt tzu nit—
Eybig geher ich nur tzu ihr aleyn,
Dos treist mir—chotsch mein tzukunft is nit sheyn.

Ven alts geht mir kapoir und alts is shlecht,
Zits ich und zorg, fun meineh tzorehs kler;
Und hob ah teineh tzu dem Oibershten—
Farvos mein mazel biter is, und shver.
Farvos bin ich nit yener vos is reich?
Tzu yener vos is sheyn, hot asach freint?
Farvos bin ich nit der vos hot talant?
Dos guts vos ich fermog, dos hob ich feint.
Azoi tracht ich, un's leben vert mir mies.
Dan mit amol, dermon ich zich on dir—
Es leitert zich mein mut, dos hartz vert gring,
Und vie ah feygeleh flieht es und zingt.
Der oisher meg zich halten mit zein gelt—
Dein liebeh is mir teier vie die velt.

I must not think of thee; and, tired yet strong,
I shun the thought that lurks in all delight—
The thought of thee—and in the blue Heaven's height,
And in the sweetest passage of a song.
O just beyond the fairest thoughts that throng
This breast, the thought of thee waits hidden yet bright;
But it must never, never come in sight;
I must stop short of thee the whole day long.
But then sleep comes to close each difficult day,
When night gives pause to the long watch I keep,
And all my bonds I need must loose apart,
Must doff my will as raiment laid away,
With the first dream that comes with the first sleep,
I run, I run, I am gathered to thy heart.

ALICE MEYNELL

Ich mus nit trachten vegen dir—neyn, nit fun dir;
Ich meid ois die gedanken fun als hertzlich—
Vie bloi der himel is, vie klor und hoich;
Vie zies und vie harmonish is ah lied.
Viebald ich fang ohn cholomen und trachten,
Meineh gedanken fliehen gleich tzu dir;
Ich mus dos nit erloiben, must viedershtehn—
Ah gantzen tog mus zich fun dir behalten.
Leyg ich zich shlofen noch ah shveren tog,
Ven nacht lozt mir zich obshtelen und ruhen—
Dan ken ich zich bereien fun die keyten
Vos halten ein mein vilen durchen tog;
Azoi vi 'skumt tzu mir der ershter driml,
Dan loif ich gleich tzu dir, tzu dir einzamlen.

# HOLIDAY VERSES

## Velvel der Tzadik

Yeder yohr, in Februahri,
Kumt ah yuntif, kein ein horeh—
Vos men kricht azh af die venten,
Tzu gefinen komplimenten.
In dem yuntifdigen nigun
Is bald yeder vort ah ligen.

"Bist ah voiler und ah sheyner,
Ah gezundt dir in die beyner.

Tiefeh kvallen deineh oigen
(Nit geshtoigen, nit gefloigen).

Veiseh perlen deineh tzeyner,
Und dein nezel is ah kleyner.

Zies vie honig is dein shmeychel;
Gor an oisnam is dein seychel.

Edel und betamt dein shtimeh—
Ohn ah shoten, ohn ah krimeh.

Ven du redst, is nor mit freyden;
Ven du zingst, is tam g'n eyden.

Dein mishpocheh und bekanteh
Zeinen zehr interresanteh.

Oi, du bist mir azoi teier—
Zeh, mein liebeh brent vie feier.

Hob rachmohnes, chaver mein,
Zei bei mir ah Valentine."

## Gershon Vashington

Rikt zich tzu ah bissel nehnter,
Hert zich ein mit grois fershtandt;
Ich vel eich dertzel'n ah meisseh
Fun dem Tateh fun mein land.

Gershon, als ah kleyner yingel,
Keyn eyn horeh, gut und voil,
Hot gehandelt nor mit emes,
Keyn eyn ligen in zein moil.

Ot tzum beishpiel, in zein gorten,
Vaxt ah kirshen-boimeleh;
Hot zich ihm ferglust, dem chochim,
Dos tzuhaken—takeh feh!

Dan tzum ovent, ven zein tateh
Fun der arbet kumt aheym,
Vert ihm finster in die oigen,
Und in hartzen ligt ah shteyn.

"Veh is mir, azah min umglik
Hot dem kirshen-boim ferchapt;
As mistameh hot ah gazlen
Dos tzushpolten und tzuhakt."

Redt zich arois der ben-yuchid,
"Lieber tateh, her zich ohn;
Oi, ich zog dir nit keyn ligen—
Dos hob ich aleyn getohn."

"Chotsh es klemt mir afen hartzen,
Und dem boimel hob ich gern,
Veil du host gezogt dem emes,
Vel ich zich nit beyzeren."

Nuzheh, yetzt is yohren shpeter,
Alles geht ihm vie geshmirt—
Vil dem Delaware ariber?
Shteht in shiffel, und men firt.

Efsher vil er zich berimmen,
As er is ah shtarker held?
Varft ah taler ibern vasser,
Veil es felt ihm nit keyn gelt.

Nu, bekitzer, alleh meiles
Hot men in dem mentsh derkent;
Hot der oilim ihm gemeldet—
"Unzer ershter President."

Shoin ah hibsheh bissel yohren,
Kleibt er kovet, noch-a-nand;
Und bei unz, zein treieh landsleit,
Heyst er "Tateh fun mein Land."

## Pincheh der Tzadik

Yeder monat hot zein yuntif,
Ven 'sis freylach afen hartzen;
Gibts ah tog—Pincheh der Tzadik,
Yeden zibentzenten fun Martzen.

Nu, mistahmeh vilt ihr vissen
Farvos kumt ihm azah shchineh?
Hot aroisgetriben shlangen
Fun die Irisheh medineh.

Fregt shoin gornit vos es tut zich—
Vie men macht fun ihm ah tzimmes;
Vie men huliyet und men hotzket—
'Ch zog eich poshet nur dem emes.

Yedeh shtundeh macht men kiddush
In die tunkeleh salunen;
Ducht zich as far alleh tzorehs
Ah refueh is gefunnen.

Kumtzheh chevreh, loz mir gehen
Zich dervaremen die glider;
Lommir oichet sheppen naches
Fun die Irisheh gebrider.

Zeh nor, zeh nor vos es tut zich,
Af die Finfteh Avenideh!
Vie men porevet zich—alleh
Oisgeputzt in farben grineh.

Her die muzik fun die klezmer,
Nigun zies vie tam g'n eyden;
Poshet ken men zich baleken
Fun die simcheh und die freyden.

Oi, ich ken zich koim einhalten!
Kuk, men fangt ohn tzu marshiren!
Der Reb Brisco geht in forent,
Fieleh toizend vet er firen.

Ot kumt Shloimeh, Chaim, Zalmen,
Velvel, Leybeleh, und Zender;
Yetzt is Mendel, Moisheh, Yankel,
Alleh voileh Irish kinder.

Shmuel, Yosel, Dovid, Chatzkel,
Azah shtoltzen fus zey shtelen;
Gershon, Yoineh, und Avromchik,
As men meg zich takeh kvellen.

Mirel, Sorkeh, Chaveh, Zlateh,
Mit die pereldikeh tzeyner;
Tzippeh, Teibeleh, und Rayzel,
Ah gezundt zey in die beyner.

Chaneh-Pessel, Esther, Yenteh,
Ot kumt Basheleh die rundeh;
Shayneh Tchipkeh, und Genendel,
In ah mazeldikeh shtundeh.

Bayleh, Frumeh, Hindeh Malkeh,
Mit die lachendikeh oigen;
Chaieh tchepet zich tzu Shayndel,
Nit geshtoigen, nit gefloigen.

Rocheleh shpatziert mit Zelig,
Ziesel halt zich ohn mit Shmeril;
Leah, Feygeleh, und Rivkeh
Ruken zich tzu Feivel, Beril.

Nu, ich ken shoin mehr nit tzeylen,
Doh faran milyonen mentshen;
Zeit gezundt, sholom aleychim,
Zol der lieber Got eich benshen.

## Oi, Friling!

Vinter kricht mir shoin fun haltzen,
Shney und frost is mir fermiest;
Vifiel is der shir tzu friren?
Glat tzu leiden is umzist.

Lieber friling, kum shoin vieder,
Kum mit grineh boimelach;
Kum mit zieseh foigel-lieder;
Kum mit sheyneh blumelach.

Af mein gas nittoh keyn boimer,
Und ah shtikel groz oich fehlt;
Nu, is boimer in die Ketskils—
Abi boimer af der velt.

Lieber friling, kum tzu loifen,
Kum mit frisheh vintelach;
Neieh hofnung velen koifen,
Die fertzarteh mentshelach.

Is bei mir nittoh keyn foigel,
'Sfelt mir zeyer pistcherei;
Vel ich tzugehn tzu Karnegi,
Dorten heren feiferei.

Lieber friling, kum tzu fliehen,
Die neshomeh geht mir ois;
Shmekedikeh duften tziehen
Fun die blumen in dein shois.

Friling is die tzeit ven yungvark
Gehn shpatzieren, hant in hant;
Die simpatisheh levoneh
Mit dem simen is bekant.

Lieber friling, heil zich shneller,
Koim ich halt ois, bei ah hohr;
Mach dos leben zieser, heller,
Shenk mir glik ah gantzen yohr.

### Nochschrift

Ver darf friling af der elter?
Vos ferdreyt ihr mir ah kop?
Meineh beyner veren kelter,
Und ich flecht ah groien tzop.

Lieber friling, zei mir moichel,
Vos ich red mit biterkeit;
'Sfelt mir ois ah bissel seychel—
'Svert ferdorben mit der tzeit.

Lieber friling, kum tzu fohren,
Deineh vunder breng mit dir;
Rateveh die letzteh yohren
Vos es zamelt zich bei mir.

## Velveleh Shakespeare

In dem sheynem monat April,
In der lieber frilings tzeit,
Gibts ah goldener geburtstog
Vos men loibt es nohnt und veit.

Lang tzurik, ah yohr fier hundert,
Hot zich dort gehodevet,
In der Englisheh medineh,
Velveleh, gebentsht fun Got.

Oi is dos geven ah shreiber
Bald der bester in der velt;
Azah oisnam is der Shakespeare—
Verter hot ihm nit gefelt.

Vilt ihr zingen? hot er lider;
Vilt ihr veynen? hot er tzar;
Glust zich eich ah bisel lachen?
Hot er ah berimten Nar.

Er hot dorten ongezamelt
Ah gedreng fun kenigen;
Und es tumult zich mit veiber,
Und mit shtoltzeh printzesin.

Nor men halt zich in eyn krigen,
Eyner hot dem tzveyten feint;
Yedeh rirung is an avleh,
Umetum die falshkeit sheint.

Ot tzum beishpiel is dort Hamlet,
Ah meshugener, ah krenk;
Hoibt er ohn komandeven, tut
Zich af tishen und af benk.

Es gefelt ihm epis gornit,
Bald ferteitsht er dos ah zind;
Mamenu  men koilet veiter,
Und dos blut vie vaser rint.

Ober Shakespeare is ah chochim,
Shreibt er vitzikeit ah sach;
Vegen vos men ruft zey fairies—
Kleyneh, voileh mentshelach.

Emis, as zey tuen mitzvehs—
Nur kapoir, nitdohgedacht;
Bei der lichtiger levoneh,
Huliyet men ah gantzeh nacht.

Und as Velveleh shreibt lider,
Perl, in zeineh shurehs ligt;
'Sis an emeseh mechayeh,
Die neshomeh vert derkvikt.

Zeineh kuntzigeh sonaten—
Azoi edel und betamt
Oi, vie er ken flechten verter!
Vu dernemt zich zein talant

Ich beereh dein geburtstog,
Lieber Velveleh Shakespeare;
Chotsh ah tropen fun dein kishuf
Zol ich yarshenen fun dir.

## Mamenu

Efsher felt eich ois ah yuntif?
Zorgt zich nit—'svet zein, 'svet zein;
Zingen vel ich eich ah liedel,
Zies vie Manischewitz vein.

Ot die meiseh hoibt zich onit
Zeks-und-fuftzig yohr tzurik;
Hoben mir ah Tog, ah sheynem,
Ful mit naches und mit glik.

In der shtedtel Philadelphy,
Vos mit mazel is gebentsht,
Hot gevoint ah voileh froikeh,
Azah oisnam fun ah mentsh.

Nemt zie trachten fun ihr mameh.
Und dos hartz hot ihr ferklemt;
Shoin ah hibsheh bissel yohren—
Und zie hot zich shtark ferbenkt.

Shteits, far als is doh ah yuntif,
Und men poret zich darin;
Nur die mameh, vos is heylig,
Ligt afileh nit in zin.

Fangt zie ohn tzu shreiben brievlach—
Nemt zie krichen af di vent—
Shtupt zich in die hoicheh fenster,
Takeh tzu dem President.

Hot zich eingeshpart, die froikeh,
Git dem Kongress nit kein ruh;
Vil der oilim zol gedenken,
As men hot ah mamenu.

Veyst ihr vos? Zie hot gepoilet—
'Sis beshtelt, in monat May,
As Got git, der tzveyter Zuntog,
Is ah yuntif—Moders Day.

Oi gevalt, is dos an oilim!
Oi is dos ah felsheh velt!
Ah gants yohr is zie vie bloteh,
Dem tog is zie vert die gelt.

Ah gants yohr is—vie se vend zich—
Men is freindlich, oder fremd;
Ober kumt tzugehn der yuntif,
Mit amol, die liebeh brent.

Kumt der Tog, shikt men ihr blumen;
Koift men Barton's shokolat;
Und men fodert zie zol essen,
Chotsh 'sken zein as zie is zat.

In die shabesdikeh kleyder,
Yeder trogt ah veiseh blum;
Men shtoltziert zich mit der mameh,
Und 'sis freylach umetum.

## Tateh Zieser

Oiben ohn, der lieber Tateh—
Nit keyn kaptzen, und nit reich;
Horevet er shver und biter—
'Svilt zich zein mit leiten gleich.

Vil bevorenen alts gutehs
Far die veib und kinderlach;
Kumt ihm takeh groiseh kovid—
Azah mentsh is vert asach.

Nu, ihr kent heintikeh kinder?
Beatniks, posheteh banditen;
Teier is bei zey der tateh?
Geht avek! Zol Got ophiten!

Men ferfinstert ihm die yohren,
Und men macht fun ihm ah shmateh;
Tomer nemt er zich beklogen,
Ligt zey in der linker piyateh.

Is doch fort ah Got in himel,
Hot zich af dem mentsh derbarimt—
Und die kinder af tzuloches,
Ihm ah Tateh-Tog bevorent.

Yetst is gor an andereh meiseh;
Itster macht men shalachmones;
Kumt tzugehn der Tog-dem-Tatens,
Shenkt men alerlei matonehs.

Shtekshich, zoken, und kravaten,
Oich ah kesteleh sigarren;
Oisgevebteh papirossen,
Tichelach fun besteh varen.

Heint is Fadders Day, ah yuntif;
Alleh kumen zich tzufohren;
Men berimt zich mit dem taten—
Es zol zein af langeh yohren.

## Hoicheh Horizanten

NIGUN: KUMT TZUM YARID

Mir machen prohjekten, entzikindig nei,
Ai, ai, kumtzheh mit uns;
Mir lerenen toireh, 'sis freylach derbei,
Ai, ai, kumtzheh mit uns.

Ferteitshen dem chumesh, die ivreh gedenk;
Ersht dan heybt zich tuen af tishen und benk.

Gloibt mir, lustig und voil, is der oilim, und froil,
Ah gedilleh!

Men geht in teyahter; kontzerten men hert—
'Sis beshert—uns—
In Horizanten, oi Horizanten, sheyn Horizanten!
Kumt zich tzugehn, lommir huliyenen—
Ai, ai, kumtzheh mit uns.

## Genug Gehorevet!

Is men reich, oder ah kaptzin;
Shtoltz, tzi nebach gor ohn statzie;
Kumt tzugehn der lieber zumer,
Yeder zucht zich ah vakatzie.

Hot men gelt? koift men ah datsheh
In die Ketskils, vu 'sis heymish;
Orim? git men zich ahn eytzeh—
Zorgen shoklen fun die pleytzeh.

Afen zamd in Kunie Eiland,
Shpringt men vie die vildeh chaies;
Oder oisgeshtrekt vie toiteh,
Bakt men zich vie burekes roiteh.

Meyleh, mentshen hoben meshugasen,
Yederer zucht zieben gliken;
Mir gefelt geradeh London,
Ihr palatzen und ihr briken.

Und die Kvien, ah voileh froikeh,
Zucht nor guts far ihr medineh;
Trogt ah kroin mit diamenten—
Vemen art dos? ich fergin ihr.

Beim palatz beit men die Shomrim,
Mit muzik und mit marshiren;
Teglich is die tzeremonyeh,
Far turistisheh gevirim.

London is ah shtodt mit gortens—
Alteh vunderlicheh boimer;
'Svaxen dort milyonen blumen—
In g'n eyden gibts nit shener.

Yeder gorten hot ah teichel
Vu men fort arum in shiffen;
Veiseh genz und roiteh katshkehs
Shvimen dort arum in miten.

In yeder heym brieht dort ah tshainik—
Kumt ah lieber gast tzugehn,
Zogt men ihm sholom aleychim,
Und derlangt ah koppatey.

Fish gebroteneh mit kartofel
Is bei zey ah gantzer meichel;
Imer mit ah glezel varems—
Ah refueh far dem beichel.

Eyn chasorin hot zie, England,
Noch-a-nand die regens tziehen;
Gradeh is dos nit ahn avleh,
Punkt ferkert—die blumen bliehen.

Amol vunder ich zich takeh,
Farvos tzieht dos hartz tzu London?
Vos is dort azah metzieh?
Nor ahin vilt zich mir fliehen.

Veyst ihr vos? 'Sis doh ah meiseh,
As dos folk vos voint dort, zeinen
Die ferloireneh neshomehs
Fun dos land fun eretz Isroel.

Oib azoi, ken men farshtehen
As dos land fermogt ah kishuf;
Und oib gelt vet mir nit fehlen,
Vel ich dorten veiter kvellen.

## Chatzkeleh  Kolumbus

Dos is ah meiseh fun amohl,
Finf hundert yohr tzurik—
Ven Chatzkeleh-fun-Genoa,
Hot uns bevorent glik.

Dos yingel est nit vetchereh,
In cheyder geht er nit;
Ah gantzen tog zitst er beim yam,
Und alleh shiffen hiet.

Is mirtchishem vaxt ois ah man,
Meshugeh, frish, gezundt;
Der akshen hot zich eingeshpart
As die velt is takeh rundt.

Bekitzer, kom mit maternish,
Gebetelt und geborgt,
Fort er tzum meirev ibern yam,
Mit drei shiffen bezorgt.

Shoin zechtzig teg men fort und fort,
Der yam is ohn ah shir;
Matrozen zeinen shtark dershrekt,
Zey shreien—"Veh is mir!

Oi Gottenu, vu first du uns?
Ven vet shoin zein an ek?
Derbarim zich, annit veln mir
Arobfallen fun breg."

Aklal, hot Got geholfen, und
Eyn sheynem inderfrieh
Hot men derzehn ah shtikel land
Zey fallen af die knee. . . .

"Geloibt zol zein der Oibershter,
Vos hot uns doh gebracht."
Fun iberrashung und fun freyd,
Hot men geveynt, gelacht.

Dos hot passiert October tzvelf,
In fiertzen-tzvey-und-ninetzig;
Tzeit dan, gibt es "Kolumbus Tog,"
Ah zehr shtoltzer yuntif.

Er hot tzvey zachen oisgefiert—
Ah neieh land gefunnen;
Zein gloiben as die velt is rundt,
Dos hot er oich gevunnen.

Es vendt zich af die umshtenden,
Und vie es sheint die shchineh—
Ven 'sis eich voil, dan is dos land
Ah Goldeneh Medineh.

Nor tomer is dos leben viest,
Men tzitert far die bombes,
'Sis biter afen hartzen, dan
"Ah klog tzu dem Kolumbus."

## Leybeleh Erikson

Oi, ah broch tzu meineh yohren—
Finster is mir in die oigen—
Dos vos ich fleg halten heylig,
Lost zich ois ah groiser ligen.

Oi, ich shtarb avek ah toiteh—
Ich ken poshet nit oishalten—
'Sligt bei mir ah shteyn in hartzen—
Ich vil shreien mit gevalten.

Gedenkt ihr Chatzkeleh Kolumbus?
Und zein velt-berimteh reizeh?
Vie er hot ah land gefunen—
Eh, 'sis gor ah bobeh-meiseh.

Gor mit fieleh doirehs frieher,
Eyder 'sis geven Kolumbus,
Zeinen dort ershinen helden—
Vikings—mener shtark vie bombes.

Groiseh, hoicheh, blondeh mentshen—
Zey fershtehen nit fun moireh—
Shtendig fort men in die shifen.
Dos is zeyer gantzeh toireh.

Und der firer fun die Vikings—
Leybeleh Erikson, heyst er,
Zamelt ein ah braveh bandeh,
Und men fort avek tzum meirev.

Vochen lang hot men gezegelt—
Vinten hoben zey fertriben—
Oisgematert, is die bandeh
In ah fremdeh land ferblieben.

Nu, bekitzer, fun die meiseh,
Kent ihr zehr gut fershtehn,
Leybel is geven der ershter
Af der neier land tzu shtehn.

Voszheh tut men mit Kolumbus?
Vemen zolen mir be-eren?
Af vos darf ich neieh tzorehs?
Farvos zol ich gisen treren?

'Sis faran azoineh leiten,
Vos zey lozen nit tzufrieden;
Ongeploidert, tzugeburtshet—
Goyim, azoi gut vie yiden.

Ot die knakers zeinen shuldig,
Zey hoben gemacht dem tumel—
Ver hot unzer land gefunen?
Is dos Chatzkel, oder Leybel?

Lozt zey klapen kop in vanten,
Fun die shtreiten vil ich lachen;
Abi dos land is mein medineh,
Abi ich ken ah leben machen.

## Halloween

Oi gevalt! shoin vider yuntif—
Ah gedilleh is af mir;
Azah tumel, ah gerider,
Und es kocht zich ohn ah shir.

Aderabeh, vos is yetzter?
Farvos is der shpigel krum?
Ah geshtrofteh machasheyfeh,
Af ah bezem flieht arum.

Ven die nacht is shtil und finster,
Und in droisen is nit gut—
Fun grois moireh vert ferglivert
In die oderen dos blut.

Plutzling hert men dort ah yammer:
Sheydim tantzen affen platz;
Shvartzeh zeveh shteht in fenster;
Af der shvell, ah shvartzeh katz.

Shkotzim punkt vie vildeh chaies—
Ongeshmirteh, grin und gel—
Shtupen, shtoisen, keren iber—
Fun als machen zey ah tel.

Ah shvartz yohr af die yungatsches—
Vie der teivel bei zey brieht;
Zey komandeven, und betlen—
Vos men ruft es "Trick or Treat."

Und men muz zey noch betzollen,
Die paskudneh chuligans;
Anit machen zey ah churben,
Vie die emeseh pogroms.

Oi, is dos mir ah medineh—
Meshugoim gibts ah sach;
Ober vu shteht es geshrieben,
Men zol hotzken affen dach?

Mayleh, als ruft zich ah simcheh—
Shreien, kvitschen, tararam;
Moichel, dreht mir nit kein spodik—
Bei mir hot es nit kein tam.

Shpeht beinacht, gut oisgematert,
Geht die chevreh zuchen ruh;
Und der oisgeplagter oilim,
Mit ah brocheh, ziftset tzu.

Sof kol sof, men lebt es iber—
Mitgemacht, aher, ahin;
Got tzu danken, obgepatert
Dem fershvartzten "Halloween."

## Tanksgivnig

Faran azah min yuntif
Vos es heyst Tanksgivnig Day;
Dos shtamt fun yeneh tzeiten
Ven dos land is vild gevehn.

M'hot nit gezehn keyn heiskelach,
Keyn gassen und keyn shtedt;
Fun teiereh depotment stores,
Is gor shoin obgeredt.

Vos ken ich eich dertzelehn
Fun die mentshen fun dos land?
Nur roiteh Indianer
Mit ah tomahok in handt.

Tzu dieseh echteh vildernish,
Drei hundert yohr tzurik,
Kumt ohn tzufohren dort ah shif—
An emeser antik.

'Sis ongepakt mit mentshen
Vos m'zucht ah neieh heym;
As chotchbeh voinen in ek velt,
Abi getrei tzu Got aleyn.

Men ruft zey epis Pilgrims,
Und zey zeinen gut und frum;
Antloifen fun der alter velt,
Doh kuken zey arum.

Aklal, der ershter vinter,
Oi, nit far eich gedacht;
'Sis nebach ah rachmohnes
Vos zey hoben mitgemacht.

Fun frosten beyz und bitter,
Fun hunger und fun tzar,
Is bald ah halber oilim
Geshtorben yenem yohr.

Tzum sof hot zich der Oibershter
Af die reshteh derbarimt;
Die neshohmeh hot er zey derkvikt,
Die glieder zey dervarimt.

Bekitzer, men hot obgelebt,
Mit naches zich bekant;
Azoi vie Got hot zey gebentsht,
Hoben zey ihm gedankt.

Simches hot men gepravet,
Maicholim ohn ah mohs;
Die Indianer eingebeten,
Tzu tcholint, tzimmis, kvas.

Tzeit dan, af yeder yohrtzeit
Fun Pilgrims, olav hasholem,
Danken mir Got—er shenkt uns
Gezundt, parnosseh, yohren.

Bei uns is oichet yuntifdig,
Men halt nur in eyn kochen;
'S tut zich af tishen und af benk,
Mit fieleh guteh zachen.

In yeder hois kumt zich tzugehn
Die teiereh mishpocheh;
Men freyt zich, und men kormet zich,
Mit mahzel und mit brocheh.

Tanksgivnig past geradeh sheyn
Die Amerikaner bieneh;
Veil Pilgrim-helden hob'n beshtelt
Die goldeneh medineh.

## Gut Yuntif

In shtodt is zehr yuntifdig,
Mit boimelach ferputzt;
Der oilim kukt ois lebedig,
Men huliyet vie fertutzt.

Men halt nur in eyn koifen,
Dos gelt rint ohn ah moss;
Vos is die groiseh simcheh?
Vos freyt men zich? Farvos?

Ah gantzen tog es tumult zich,
Mit zmirehs ohn ah shir;
Men ruft es epis "kerils,"
Ah gedileh is af mir.

Ah zingenish, ah klingenish,
Men darf es af kaporehs;
Ich mish zich nit in goi-ishkeit,
Ich hob mein eygeneh tzorehs.

As mirtshishem antloift die tzeit,
M'hot krismes obgepatert,
Dan bleibt der oilim vie entoisht,
Ferorimt und fermatert.

Yuntoivim fliehen shnel avek—
Azoi fergehn die yohren;
Abi gezundt, mein lieber freind,
Es zol eich gornit ahren.

Parnosseh, naches, vinsh ich eich,
Es zol eich voil bekumen;
Und vu ihr gibt zich nor ah kehr,
Ah gorten full mit blumen.

## Gut Yohr

In die letzteh teg, Decembers,
Fangt der oilim zich tzu pohren;
Balebatish, vie es past zich,
Einladen die neieh yohren.

Kosher is er nit, der yuntif,
Mitzvehs vet men nit ferdinen;
Mentshen machen zich meshugeh—
Men geht glat arop fun zinen.

Meyleh, es is nit keyn avleh
As men vil annoyeh hoben;
Chotsh eyn tog zich amuziren,
Alleh veytiken begroben.

Kumt beinacht, um tzvelf azeyger,
Lozt zich plutzling ois der boidim;
Klingen, feifen, kvitshen, shreien,
Men gevaltiget vie sheydim.

Gelt is bilig heint, vie bloteh,
Men fernutzt es, gleich vie gornit;
M'hot beganvet yeden knipel,
Yedeh pushkeh oisgeleydikt.

Vie men shikert und men huliyet!
Vie men macht azah gerider
Vieder nochamol ah shnepsil—
Alleh zeinen voileh brider.

Zeitzheh lustig, zeitzheh freylach—
Nit gedeiget vegen morgen;
Heppy New Year! Skol! L'chaim!
Und af morgen zol Got zorgen.